Student Applications Book

Great Source Education Group
a Houghton Mifflin Company
Wilmington, Massachusetts

www.greatsource.com

AUTHORS

Laura Robb
Author

Powhatan School, Boyce, Virginia
Laura Robb, author of *Reading Strategies That Work* and *Teaching Reading in Middle School,* has taught Language Arts at Powhatan School in Boyce, Virginia, for more than 30 years. She is a co-author of the *Reading and Writing Sourcebooks* for grades 3–5 and the *Summer Success: Reading* program. Robb also mentors and coaches teachers in Virginia public schools and speaks at conferences throughout the country on reading and writing.

Margaret Ann Richek
Contributing Author

Northeastern Illinois University, Chicago, Illinois
Margaret Ann Richek is a professor of education at Northeastern Illinois University. Her specialty is the teaching of reading. She is a former teacher in Chicago and the metropolitan Chicago area. She consults extensively for school districts. Her publications include a series of ten co-authored books, *Vocabulary for Achievement* (Grades 3-10), *The World of Words: Vocabulary for College Students*, and a co-authored text, *Reading Problems: Assessment and Teaching Strategies*. Her work is also featured in *Vocabulary Strategies That Boost Students' Reading Comprehension*.

Vicki Spandel
Contributing Author

Writing specialist Vicki Spandel was co-director of the 17-member teaching team that developed the 6-trait model for writing instruction and assessment. She is the author of more than 30 books for students and teachers, including *Daybooks of Critical Reading and Writing* (for grades 3-5) and *Write Traits Classroom Kits*. Vicki has been a language arts teacher, award-winning video producer, technical writer, journalist, freelance editor, and scoring director for numerous writing assessments. As lead trainer for Write Traits, she works as a writing consultant and visiting teacher throughout the country and develops a wide range of instructional materials for use in grades K-12.

Editorial:
Design:
Illustrations:

Developed by Nieman, Inc. with Phil LaLeike
Ronan Design: Christine Ronan, Sean O'Neill, Maria Mariottini, Victoria Mullins
Mike McConnell

Trademarks and trade names are shown in this book strictly for illustrative purposes and are the property of their respective owners. The author's references herein should not be regarded as affecting their validity.

Copyright © 2002 by Great Source Education Group, Inc. All rights reserved.
Great Source® is a registered trademark of Houghton Mifflin Company.

Permission is hereby granted to teachers who have purchased the *Reader's Handbook* and the Complete Program Package (Grade 5, ISBN 0-669-49533-6) to reprint or photocopy in classroom quantities the pages or sheets in this work that carry a copyright notice, provided each copy made shows the copyright notice. Such copies may not be sold and further distribution is expressly prohibited. Except as authorized above, prior written permission must be obtained from Great Source Education Group, Inc., to reproduce or transmit this work or portions thereof in any other form or by any other electronic or mechanical means, including any information storage or retrieval system, unless expressly permitted by federal copyright law. Address inquiries to Great Source Education Group, Inc., 181 Ballardvale Street, Wilmington, Massachusetts 01887.

Printed in the United States of America

International Standard Book Number: 0-669-49529-8
(Student Applications Book)

1 2 3 4 5 6 7 8 9—DBH—08 07 06 05 04 03 02

International Standard Book Number: 0-669-49531-X
(Student Applications Book, Teacher's Edition)

1 2 3 4 5 6 7 8 9—DBH—08 07 06 05 04 03 02

Table of Contents

What Happens When You Read

The first step to becoming a better reader is to understand your own reading habits. Think about what you read in a given day. Where, when, and why do you read? What's your purpose? Make a few notes here.

What you read.

Sometimes you read for school. Sometimes you read for pleasure. Other times, you read without even knowing it.

Directions: Think about everything you read yesterday. Make a list here. Then compare your list with that of a classmate.

List

I read these things yesterday:

street signs on the way to school

© GREAT SOURCE. ALL RIGHTS RESERVED.

Why you read.

Page 23 of the *Reader's Handbook* suggests six good reasons for reading. What reasons can you add to this list?

Directions: On the lines below, list six reasons for reading. (We've done the first one for you.) Then explain each.

◀ **List**

Here are six reasons why I read:

1. I read for enjoyment

   because I like to get caught up in a good book.

2. I read

   because

3. I read

   because

4. I read

   because

5. I read

   because

6. I read

   because

© GREAT SOURCE. ALL RIGHTS RESERVED.

NAME ....

FOR USE WITH PAGES 23–25

See yourself reading.

You may not know it, but reading is a process. Each time you read, you follow a series of important steps. Becoming a better reader involves understanding the steps in this process.

Directions: Draw a picture of yourself reading a really great book. Use "balloons" to show what you are thinking.

This is me reading.

© GREAT SOURCE. ALL RIGHTS RESERVED.

Ask questions about what you read.

What do you think about as you read? What questions do you ask yourself?

Directions: Choose a book from the classroom library that you want to read this school year. Write the title and author's name on the lines. Then ask and answer some questions about the book you've chosen.

Title:

Author's Name:

What is the book about?

Why are you reading?

What do you want to get out of your reading?

What kind of reading is it?

Should you read slowly or quickly?

What can you do if you don't understand something?

How can you remember what you've read?

How do you know if you've understood it?

Will you read it more than once?

© GREAT SOURCE. ALL RIGHTS RESERVED.

The Reading Process

Think of the reading process as the steps you follow to get more from a text.

Your Reading Process

Everyone has his or her own habits when it comes to reading. What are yours? What is *your* reading process?

Directions: Tell what you do before, during, and after reading. Make notes or write in full sentences.

Before Reading

I _____

_____

_____

During Reading

I _____

_____

_____

After Reading

I _____

_____

_____

© GREAT SOURCE. ALL RIGHTS RESERVED.

NAME ....

FOR USE WITH PAGES 28–33

The Handbook's Reading Process

The reading process is a little like a road map. Use it to prevent yourself from getting lost in a text.

Directions: Skim pages 28–33. Look at the steps in the reading process. Summarize these steps on the lines below.

Before Reading

....

....

....

....

During Reading

....

....

....

....

After Reading

....

....

....

....

....

© GREAT SOURCE. ALL RIGHTS RESERVED.

If you get stuck, look at the Summing Up section on page 33 of the handbook.

Reading  Know-how

You have years and years of reading tips, ideas, and strategies all stored in your brain. Now it's time to put this information to use. Begin by sharpening your critical thinking skills.

Thinking Skill 1: Making Inferences

No writer will tell you everything. Some things you'll need to figure out on your own. This means reading between the lines and making inferences.

Directions: Read the paragraph in the box. Then use your inferences to help you answer the questions that follow.

> ### Sample Paragraph
>
> The school is brightly lit, even though it is 7:00 P.M. Parents rush from the parking lot into the front door. Student ushers direct them to the gym. Inside the gym, there are 100 folding chairs set up in rows. All the teachers in the school sit up front, facing the chairs. The principal stands at the podium and waits for the crowd to settle down. A large poster hangs on the wall near the principal. It says:
>
> **Welcome Parents!!!!**
>
> Raise your hand if you're looking forward to a great school year!

My Inferences

Circle one.

Parents have come to the school for: a school board meeting or back-to-school night.

How I know this:

Circle one.

The principal stands in front because: she is going to speak or there is no seat left for her.

How I know this:

© GREAT SOURCE. ALL RIGHTS RESERVED.

My Inferences

Circle one.

The teachers are there to: meet the parents or keep an eye on the student ushers.

How I know this:

Thinking Skill 2: Drawing Conclusions

When you draw conclusions, you look at the facts and then decide what they mean. Drawing conclusions is putting two and two together to get four.

Drawing Conclusions Chart

Fact 1

Fact 2

Fact 3

Fact 4

Conclusion

© GREAT SOURCE. ALL RIGHTS RESERVED.

Thinking Skill 3: Comparing and Contrasting

When you compare and contrast, you think about the ways in which two things are alike and different.

Directions: Put two books on your desk. Compare their size, shape, thickness, and appearance. Write your notes on this Venn Diagram.

Venn Diagram

Write notes that describe Book A here.

Write notes that describe Book B here.

Book A Title:

Both

Book B Title:

Write what they have in common.

Thinking Skill 4: Evaluating

Evaluating is making a judgment or giving an opinion. It means saying what you do and don't like about something.

Directions: Take another look at the two books sitting in front of you. Which book looks more interesting? Explain your opinion.

Write a book title here.

I think _____ looks more interesting because _____

....

© GREAT SOURCE. ALL RIGHTS RESERVED.

Thinking Skill 5: Predicting

When you read, you make predictions. This means you guess what will happen next based on what you've read and your own experience.

Directions: Think about yourself as a reader. Then make some predictions about this *Student Applications Book*.

Predicting Chart

Here's what I know about myself as a reader:	• I predict this book will help me
	• I think the questions will be easy/hard to answer. Here's why:
	• I predict I will/will not enjoy completing the activities. Here's why:

Pulling It All Together

All five critical thinking skills will come in handy as you learn to become a better reader.

Directions: Make a list of the five important thinking skills. Tell how you think each skill can help you become a better reader.

Thinking Skill 1: ....

Thinking Skill 2: ....

Thinking Skill 3: ....

....

Thinking Skill 4: ....

Thinking Skill 5: ....

© GREAT SOURCE. ALL RIGHTS RESERVED.

Reading Actively

Active readers throw themselves into a text. They ask questions, make predictions, and hold "conversations" with the author. They keep at it until they understand what they're reading.

Ways of Reading Actively

Good readers mark a text as they read. They jot down their comments and make sketches. They read *actively,* rather than *passively.*

Directions: Turn to page 40 of your handbook. Read the section called "Six Ways to Read Actively." Then do an active reading of these paragraphs from a novel.

from *Freaky Friday* by Mary Rodgers

You are not going to believe me, nobody in their right minds could *possibly* believe me, but it's true, really it is!

When I woke up this morning, I found I'd turned into my mother. There I was, in my mother's bed, with my feet reaching all the way to the bottom, and my father sleeping in the other bed. I had on my mother's nightgown, and a ring on my left hand, I mean her left hand, and lumps and pins all over my head.

"I think that must be the rollers," I said to myself, "and if I have my mother's hair, I probably have her face, too."

I decided to take a look at myself in the bathroom mirror. After all, you don't turn into your mother every day of the week; maybe I was imagining it—or dreaming.

Well, I wasn't. What I saw in that mirror was absolutely my mother from top to toe, complete with no braces on the teeth. Now ordinarily, I don't bother to brush too often—it's a big nuisance with all those wires—but my mother's teeth looked like a fun job, and besides, if she was willing to do a terrific thing like turning her body over to me like that, the least I could do was take care of her teeth for *her.* Right? Right.

1. Mark

Underline information about time and place.

© GREAT SOURCE. ALL RIGHTS RESERVED.

2. React and Connect

Tell how you would feel if you were

in the narrator's shoes.

3. Question

Ask a question about the

plot here.

5. Make Things Clear

Tell what you've learned so far about

the story.

4. Create Pictures

Make a sketch of the scene here.

6. Predict

Predict what the main problem in this

novel will be.

© GREAT SOURCE. ALL RIGHTS RESERVED.

Reading Paragraphs

Finding the main idea of a paragraph—and figuring out what it means—is one of your most important jobs as a reader. Follow these steps to analyze a paragraph.

Step 1: Read.

First, do an active reading of the paragraph. As you read, ask yourself, "What is the subject of this paragraph?"

Directions: Read this paragraph from a famous speech. Highlight important words and phrases. Make notes on the stickies.

from "But We Shall Sell No More," a speech by Chief Metea

My Father, we have sold you a great tract of land already; but it is not enough! We sold it to you for the benefit of your children, to farm and to live upon. We have now but a little left. We shall want it all for ourselves. We know not how long we shall live, and we wish to leave some lands for our children to hunt upon. You are gradually taking away our hunting grounds. Your children are driving us before them. We are growing uneasy. What lands you have you may retain. But we shall sell no more.

Clarify

Who do you think is Metea's audience for this speech?

Highlight/Mark

Ask and answer this question: What is Metea talking about in this paragraph?

© GREAT SOURCE. ALL RIGHTS RESERVED.

Step 2: Find the subject.

Next, find the subject of the paragraph. You can find clues about the subject by looking at these items.

◄ **Subject Checklist** ━━━━━━━━━━━━━━━━━━━━━━━━━━━━━

☐ Title

☐ First and last sentences

☐ Repeated words and phrases

Directions: Answer these questions. They can help you find the subject of the paragraph from Metea's speech.

What is the title of the selection?
....

What is the first sentence about?
....

....

What repeated words and phrases did you notice?
....

What would you say is the subject of the paragraph?
....

Step 3: Find the main idea.

The main idea is what the writer is saying about the subject. Some paragraphs have a stated main idea. In other paragraphs, the main idea is implied.

Stated Main Idea Some authors make a direct statement about the main idea. Very often the stated main idea will be located in the first or last sentence of the paragraph.

Directions: Reread the first and last sentences of the Chief Metea paragraph. Then write his main idea on the lines below.

The main idea of the paragraph is
....

Implied Main Idea Sometimes the main idea of a paragraph is implied. This means it's not directly stated. When this is the case, you must make inferences about the main idea. To make an inference about the main idea, ask yourself, "What is the writer trying to tell me about the subject?"

© GREAT SOURCE. ALL RIGHTS RESERVED.

Directions: Reflect on Metea's speech. Then write your answer to the question that follows.

What is Metea trying to tell his audience about the white man's government?

Step 4: Find support for the main idea.

Good writers support a main idea with strong facts and details. A main idea organizer can help you see how the main idea and details work together in a paragraph.

Directions: Complete this organizer. Refer to your notes as needed.

Main Idea Organizer

Topic:		
Stated Main Idea:		
Detail 1	**Detail 2**	**Detail 3**

Write three details from the speech that support Metea's main idea.

© GREAT SOURCE. ALL RIGHTS RESERVED.

Reading Social Studies

A social studies textbook gives you information about a historical period. The articles, pictures, maps, and diagrams in the book are there to help you picture what life was like during that period. When reading social studies, your job is to keep track of the facts, ideas, and terms discussed in each chapter. Use the reading process to help you do this.

Before Reading

Use the reading process and the strategy of using graphic organizers to help you read and understand a social studies chapter called "Reconstruction: The First Year."

A Set a Purpose

Your purpose when reading social studies is to learn facts about the subject. You also should think about how the subject relates to you personally.

• **To set your purpose, ask two questions about the chapter title.**

Directions: Write two purpose questions about the social studies chapter "Reconstruction: The First Year."

◄ **My Questions**

Question #1: ....

....

....

Question #2: ....

....

....

© GREAT SOURCE. ALL RIGHTS RESERVED.

B Preview

Always begin with a preview. As you preview, watch for information about the subject of the chapter.

Directions: Run your eyes over the social studies chapter that follows on pages 23–26. Make notes on this chart.

Preview Chart

Questions	My Notes
What is the title of the chapter?	
What is the subject?	
What boldface terms did you see?	
What did you notice about the pictures?	
What were the questions at the end of the chapter like?	

© GREAT SOURCE. ALL RIGHTS RESERVED.

9 Reconstruction:
THE FIRST YEAR

Textbooks

Key Terms

plantation
assemble
amendment
Freedman's
  Bureau
Reconstruction
punitive
militia
black codes

Study Guide

Main Idea: Rebuilding the nation after the Civil War was a long and difficult process.

Goals: As you read, look for answers to these questions:
- What was the Thirteenth Amendment to the Constitution?
- What was the purpose of the Freedman's Bureau?
- Why were African Americans so upset by the black codes?

Ten-year-old Selma Rose worked fourteen hours a day in the big house of the Jepson's Tennessee **plantation.** Because she had been born a slave, Selma worked six days a week—without wages and without the chance to go to school to learn to read and write. Although her mother told her to never give up hope, Selma had stopped dreaming about freedom. She was sure she would be a slave for her whole life.

In just one afternoon in 1865, however, Selma's life changed forever. That day, as Selma was preparing the noontime meal, a group of soldiers rode up on horseback. They asked Selma to ring the plantation bell long and hard. They wanted to signal the slaves to leave their work and **assemble,** or meet, at the big house.

One by one, the men and women who worked the Jepson plantation made their way up to the house. After the last had arrived, the white men made a startling announcement: "You're free, now. The war is over and so is slavery. You are as free as any white man or woman in the country."

Stop and Record
Make notes in the "end of Slavery" section of your Web on page 27.

© GREAT SOURCE. ALL RIGHTS RESERVED.

Some men and women burst into tears at the news. Some fell to their knees to give thanks. Others, like Selma, simply repeated again and again the words that they had been waiting so long to hear: "Free! At long last, we're free!"

New Beginnings

Like millions of other African Americans, the slaves on the Jepson plantation won their freedom with the South's defeat in the Civil War. In 1865, their freedom was guaranteed with the passage of the Thirteenth Amendment to the United States Constitution. This **amendment,** or change, to the Constitution proclaimed to the world that slavery was forever abolished in the United States.

For African Americans in the South, it was a chance to create a new life—to forge a new beginning. Although the South lay in ruins, President Lincoln had promised to give land to the blacks after the war ended.

As a first step, Lincoln directed Congress to set up what would become known as the **Freedman's Bureau.** The purpose of the Freedman's Bureau was to help African Americans get the schooling they so desperately wanted. The process of building a new and better South had begun.

Students and teachers pose outside the Freedman's Bureau school on Edisto Island, South Carolina, ca. 1865.

Stop and Record

Make some notes in the "President Lincoln" part of your Web on page 27.

© GREAT SOURCE. ALL RIGHTS RESERVED.

Reconstruction

Unfortunately, the problem of how best to help the newly freed African Americans was only one of the many problems facing the nation as the Civil War drew to a close. In private, Lincoln confided that he was deeply worried about the state of the Union. Whole cities had been burnt to the ground during the war, and millions of acres of farmland had been destroyed. Worse yet, close to 620,000 soldiers had died in the war. The entire nation was almost paralyzed by grief.

In the final months of the war, Lincoln spoke to as many Americans as he could. He explained that what the country needed was a tremendous period of **reconstruction,** or rebuilding. The purpose of this reconstruction period, Lincoln said, would be to reunite North and South to form a single union. To aid in the healing, there would be no **punitive,** or punishing, measures taken against the South. The American people had suffered enough.

Conflict over Reuniting

The twelve years that came after the Civil War—now known as the Reconstruction period— were indeed years of rebuilding. Yet, reuniting North and South was more difficult than Lincoln ever imagined.

The first blow came with Lincoln's assassination in April of 1865. Lincoln's successor, President Andrew Johnson, was a Southerner at heart. He had his own ideas of how to bring the Confederate states back into the Union. Johnson's plan offered few rights and little freedom to the newly freed African American slaves.

President Andrew Johnson

Stop and Record
Make notes in the "President Johnson" part of your Web on page 27.

© GREAT SOURCE. ALL RIGHTS RESERVED.

One of the first things Johnson did as President was to pardon a number of Southern leaders, including Confederate officials and army officers who had served in the war. He then directed the former Confederates to establish new state governments in the South.

Almost immediately, the new Southern governments adopted a number of laws designed to keep former slaves from voting, testifying against whites in court, and joining the **militia** (state army forces). These laws, which were known as **black codes,** severely limited the freedom of African Americans living in the South. Many men and women felt they had been enslaved all over again.

Stop and Record

Make notes in "the black codes" part of your Web on page 27.

Social Studies Check Point

1. What was Reconstruction?
2. Explain the Thirteenth Amendment to the Constitution. How did these Amendments help men and women held as slaves in the South?

C Plan

The strategy of using graphic organizers can help you sort through the facts in a social studies chapter.

• **Write notes on a graphic organizer as you read. This will help you keep track of important details.**

© GREAT SOURCE. ALL RIGHTS RESERVED.

During Reading

Now go back and do a careful reading of "Reconstruction: The First Year." Use a graphic organizer to keep track of your notes.

D Read with a Purpose

A Web can help you see connections between different ideas and details in a chapter.

Directions: Make notes on this Web as you read.

© GREAT SOURCE. ALL RIGHTS RESERVED.

Textbooks

Web

the end of slavery

President Lincoln

The first year of Reconstruction

President Johnson

the black codes

Using the Strategy

All kinds of graphic organizers work well with a social studies text.

• **Key Word or Topic Notes can help you get a handle on the most important ideas in a chapter.**

Directions: Read the list of topics in Column 1. Write your notes from the chapter in Column 2.

Key Word or Topic Notes

Key Words	My Notes
the end of slavery 1865	
President Lincoln	
Reconstruction	
President Johnson	
the black codes	

© GREAT SOURCE. ALL RIGHTS RESERVED.

Understanding How Social Studies Textbooks Are Organized

Many social studies chapters open with a study guide or "goals" box. Use the information in this box to help you understand the most important details in the chapter.

Key Terms
• • • • • • • • • • • • • • •
plantation
assemble
amendment
Freedman's
    Bureau
reconstruction
punitive
militia
black codes

Study Guide

Main Idea: Rebuilding the nation after the Civil War was a long and difficult process.

Goals: As you read, look for answers to these questions:
• What was the Thirteenth Amendment to the Constitution?
• What was the purpose of the Freedman's Bureau?
• Why were African Americans so upset by the black codes?

Directions: Answer the questions under "Goals" in the Study Guide. Then define the key terms.

Study Guide Questions

1. What was the Thirteenth Amendment to the Constitution?

2. What was the purpose of the Freedman's Bureau?

3. Why were African Americans so upset about the black codes?

© GREAT SOURCE. ALL RIGHTS RESERVED.

Textbooks

Definitions of Key Terms

plantation—

assemble—

amendment—

Freedman's Bureau—

Reconstruction—

punitive—

militia—

black codes—

 **E Connect**

When you make a connection to a text, you ask yourself questions about what you've read and learned.

- **Connecting to a social studies text can make the facts and details seem more real to you.**

© GREAT SOURCE. ALL RIGHTS RESERVED.

Directions: Answer the questions on these stickies.

Connection Questions

How did the information in the chapter make you feel?

What else have you read that reminds you of this chapter?

After Reading

After you finish reading, think about what you've learned.

F Pause and Reflect

Return to your preview questions. Are you able to answer them now?

• **Ask yourself, "Have I met my purpose?"**

Directions: Write your purpose questions from page 21 on the lines below. Then answer them.

Question #1:

My answer:

Question #2:

My answer:

G Reread

The rereading strategy of finding cause and effect can help you make links between events and ideas in history.

© GREAT SOURCE. ALL RIGHTS RESERVED.

- **Use a Cause-Effect Organizer to help you think about the most important ideas in the chapter.**

Directions: Complete this Cause-Effect Organizer. Refer to your notes and the reading.

Cause-Effect Organizer

Effects

Cause

Lincoln frees the slaves.

H Remember

It's important to remember what you learn in social studies. You will surely need the information some time in the future.

- **Making a personal connection to the information can help you remember it.**

Directions: Write a journal entry about Reconstruction in your notebook. Include questions you have about the topic and where you might go for answers.

Journal Entry

© GREAT SOURCE. ALL RIGHTS RESERVED.

NAME _____

Reading Science

Reading science involves asking how and why something has occurred. It also means learning new terms and facts. Use the tools and strategies described in the handbook to help you understand what you're reading.

Before Reading

Use the strategy of note-taking to help you get *more* from a science chapter.

A Set a Purpose

Your purpose for reading science is to learn everything you can about the subject.

> • **To set your purpose, ask a question about the subject of the chapter.**

Directions: Write your purpose for reading "The Five Kingdoms" here. Then make a prediction about the chapter. What do you expect to learn?

My purpose: ....

....

....

....

I think the reading will be about: ....

....

....

....

© GREAT SOURCE. ALL RIGHTS RESERVED.

B Preview

On your preview, look for information about the subject of the chapter. Try to get a sense of what you'll be learning as you read.

Directions: Preview the science chapter that follows. Place a check mark beside each item on the list as you look at it. Then make some notes on the chart below.

Preview Checklist

☐ Title and subheadings

☐ Boxed items

☐ Words in boldface

☐ Any photos, maps, diagrams, and so on

☐ First and last paragraphs

Preview Chart

The titles and headings tell me . . .	I noticed these boldface words . . .

The Five Kingdoms

The art tells me . . .	The first and last paragraphs tell me . . .

© GREAT SOURCE. ALL RIGHTS RESERVED.

NAME ....

FOR USE WITH PAGES 74–87

Textbooks

Chapter

2

The Five Kingdoms

Did you know that more than two million kinds of living things have been identified to date? To keep track of this huge number, scientists have long **classified,** or sorted, all living things into five large categories, called **kingdoms.** The organisms in each of the five kingdoms share some important characteristics.

Kingdom Monera

The smallest and simplest life forms on earth are in the kingdom Monera. **Monerans** are very tiny, one-celled, and often live in chains or groups (see Figure 2.1). Bacteria, for example, are in the kingdom Monera. Unlike all other living things, moneran cells have no nucleus. To survive, most monerans take in food from their environment. One exception is cyanobacteria, which make their own food using **chlorophyll,** the substance used by plants for food production.

> **GUIDE FOR READING**
>
> **GOALS**
> 1. Learn the names and characteristics of the five kingdoms.
> 2. Understand how different organisms are classified into different kingdoms.
>
> **KEY TERMS**
> classified   organelles
> kingdoms   spores
> monerans   photosynthesis
> chlorophyll   invertebrates
> protists   vertebrates
>
> **SCIENCE ALERT!**
> Sometime in the next several years, scientists may add a sixth kingdom. New discoveries about monerans have led scientists to believe that this grouping should actually be split into two different kingdoms.

Figure 2.1: *Bacilli, rod-shaped bacteria*

© GREAT SOURCE. ALL RIGHTS RESERVED.

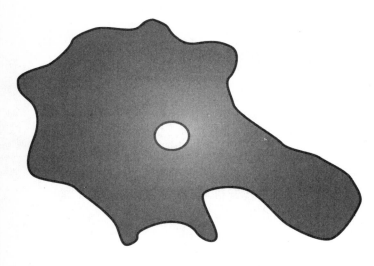

Figure 2.2: *Amoeba, a one-celled protozoan.*

Kingdom Protista

The kingdom Protista also contains one-celled microorganisms, although **protists** are not as simple as the single-celled monerans. All protist cells contain a nucleus and other **organelles,** which are structures that control the cell. The protists are divided into several groups that share characteristics. These include diatoms, protozoans, algae, and amoebas (Figure 2.2).

Kingdom Fungi

Most members of the kingdom Fungi are multicellular organisms with complex cell structures and cell walls. The organisms in this kingdom do not make chlorophyll, so they are unable to make their own food. Instead, fungi use chemicals to dissolve their food and then absorb it. Fungi are also unique because they reproduce through **spores,** tiny bodies that can grow into new organisms. Molds, mildews, rusts, and mushrooms are all a part of the kingdom Fungi (Figure 2.3).

Figure 2.3: *Mushroom.*

© GREAT SOURCE. ALL RIGHTS RESERVED.

Kingdom Plantae

Members of the kingdom Plantae are often bigger and can live longer than any other species on earth. These organisms are multicellular. They have rigid cell walls that contain cellulose. Species in this kingdom make their own food using a process known as **photosynthesis.** Flowering plants, trees, mosses, and ferns are all a part of the kingdom Plantae (Figure 2.4).

Kingdom Animalia

The kingdom Animalia contains multicellular animals that cannot make their own food. The animal kingdom is often divided into two major groupings: **invertebrates** (animals with no backbone) and **vertebrates** (animals with backbones). Invertebrates include worms, insects, oysters, and sponges (Figure 2.5). Vertebrates include fish, amphibians, reptiles, birds, mammals, and humans.

Figure 2.4: *The kingdom Plantae includes flowering plants, trees, mosses, and ferns.*

Figure 2.5: *Did you know that sponges are part of the kingdom Animalia?*

© GREAT SOURCE. ALL RIGHTS RESERVED.

C Plan

After previewing the chapter, make a plan. Choose a strategy that can help you read, understand, and remember what you've learned.

• Use the strategy of note-taking to get *more* from a science text.

During Reading

D Read with a Purpose

Remember that your purpose is to find out as much as you can about the topic discussed in the chapter.

Directions: Now do a close reading of the chapter. Use this Web for your notes.

Web

The Five Kingdoms

© GREAT SOURCE. ALL RIGHTS RESERVED.

NAME ....

Using the Strategy

Thumb through the Reading Tools section of your handbook. Many of the tools described here will work well with the strategy of note-taking.

- **Choose a tool that will help you organize the notes you made while reading.**

Directions: Make notes about the kingdom Monera on this Concept Map. When you finish, make Concept Maps for the other four kingdoms. Keep these maps in your science notebook.

Concept Map

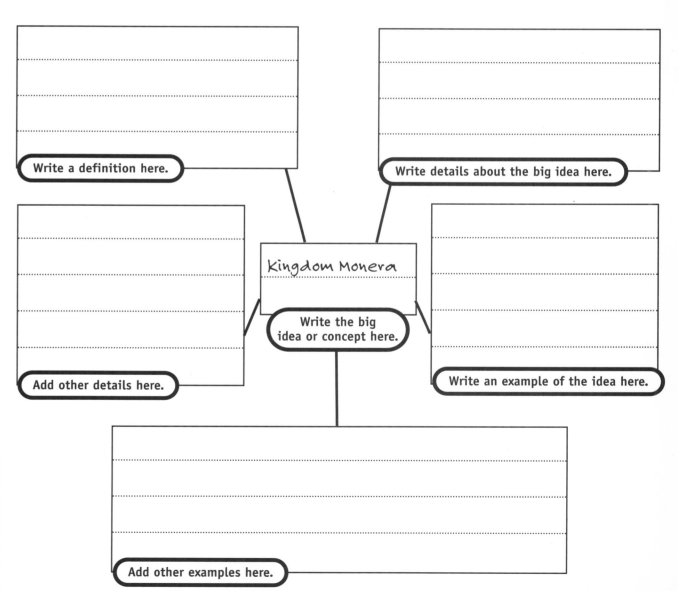

Write a definition here.

Write details about the big idea here.

Kingdom Monera

Write the big idea or concept here.

Add other details here.

Write an example of the idea here.

Add other examples here.

© GREAT SOURCE. ALL RIGHTS RESERVED.

Understanding How Science Textbooks Are Organized

Some of the chapters in your science text will discuss how things are grouped or classified. Summary Notes can help you see how the individual groups work together.

Directions: Make Summary Notes about the five kingdoms.

Summary Notes

Title:

Main point:

> Write four or five smaller related points that support the main idea here.

1.

2.

3.

4.

5.

E Connect

A science chapter will be easier to read and understand if you can make a personal connection to the topic.

• **Ask yourself, "What is most interesting about the reading?" or "How do these ideas explain what I see?"**

Directions: Write your reactions to "The Five Kingdoms."

This is what I found most interesting:

© GREAT SOURCE. ALL RIGHTS RESERVED.

After Reading

Be sure you understand what you've read before moving on to another chapter or assignment.

F Pause and Reflect

Return to your reading purpose and ask yourself what you've learned about the topic.

- **After you finish reading, ask yourself, "Did I meet my purpose?"**

Directions: Answer *yes* or *no* to these questions.

Do I know the main topic of the chapter? ....

Can I explain the topic in my own words? ....

Can I explain the key terms? ....

Do the graphics, pictures, and captions make sense to me? ....

G Reread

Do some rereading if you can't answer *yes* to each of the questions.

- **The rereading strategy of paraphrasing can help you "absorb" additional information.**

Directions: Paraphrase what you've learned about the five kingdoms.

Paraphrase Chart

....

....

....

....

....

....

....

© GREAT SOURCE. ALL RIGHTS RESERVED.

Textbooks

Remember

Making a sketch can help you remember what you've learned.

• **To help you remember a science chapter, make a sketch.**

Directions: Draw one organism from each kingdom.

Monera	Protista

Fungi	Plantae	Animalia

© GREAT SOURCE. ALL RIGHTS RESERVED.

Reading  Math

Your math textbook is filled with all kinds of things to read: numbers, symbols, word problems, directions, rules, explanations, and so much more. The reading process can help.

Before Reading

Practice reading a math text here. Use the strategy of visualizing and thinking aloud to help you understand what you read.

A Set a Purpose

It's easy to set a purpose for reading math. Simply turn the chapter or article title into a question, and make that question your purpose for reading.

• To set your purpose, ask a question about the chapter title.

Directions: Write your purpose for reading a math chapter called "Metric Measurement." Then tell what you already know about this subject.

My purpose: ....

....

....

The easiest part will be: ....

....

....

The hardest part will be: ....

....

© GREAT SOURCE. ALL RIGHTS RESERVED.

B Preview

Once you've set your purpose, begin previewing. Look for the subject of the chapter. Pay attention to the directions, examples, and explanations.

• Use a K-W-L Chart for your preview notes.

Directions: Preview the two math pages that follow. Look for the items on this checklist. Then make notes on the K-W-L Chart.

Preview Checklist

- ☐ Chapter title and any subtitles
- ☐ Key terms
- ☐ Boxed items
- ☐ Sample problems
- ☐ Practice problems

K-W-L Chart

What I **K**now	What I **W**ant to Know	What I **L**earned

Write what you already know about the subject here.

Write what you need to find out about the subject here.

Make notes here after your careful reading.

© GREAT SOURCE. ALL RIGHTS RESERVED.

Chapter 11 Metric Measurement

Textbooks

Goal 1 Learn to measure an object in centimeters and decimeters.

The **centimeter, decimeter,** and **meter** are metric units of length. You can use them to measure both length and width. Their abbreviations are cm, dm, and m.

$$1 \text{ dm} = 10 \text{ cm}$$
$$1 \text{ m} = 10 \text{ dm}$$

FIND OUT: Name a unit of metric measurement that is *smaller* than a centimeter.

You can use the centimeters, decimeters, and meters to find measurement the same way you use inches, feet, and yards.

The **kilometer** (km) is also a metric unit of length. A kilometer is about the same length as five city blocks. Most people can walk a kilometer in just under ten minutes.

$$1 \text{ km} = 1,000 \text{ m}$$

FIND OUT: Name a unit of metric measurement that is *larger* than a kilometer.

Goals

Learn to measure the length of an object in centimeters and decimeters.
Estimate the length or width of an object in meters and kilometers.

Key Terms

centimeter
decimeter
meter
estimate
kilometer

DOUBLE-CHECK √√ **Centimeters, Decimeters, Meters**
Directions: Measure the length of these objects in centimeters and decimeters. Record your answers.
1. The *Reader's Handbook*   3. your desk top
2. your arm   4. the distance from your seat to the door

How large is a decimeter?

How large is a kilometer?

Directions For each pair of measurements below, tell which is longer or if both are the same length.

5. 4 m	6. 8 dm	7. 10 dm	8. 9,000 m
3 km	2 m	100 cm	10 km

© GREAT SOURCE. ALL RIGHTS RESERVED.

Goal 2 Estimate the length or width of an object in meters and kilometers.

Some things are too large to be measured by a metric ruler or tape measure. You have to **estimate** (find a number close to the exact amount) the length or width of these objects.

DOUBLE-CHECK √√ **Estimating Length and Width**

Directions: Estimate the height or width of each of these objects.

1. 2 m
  2 km

2. 15 m
  15 km

3. 3 m
  3 km

Directions Tell if the width is <u>greater</u> or <u>less than</u> 1 km.

4. 4,000 m ....

5. 1,500 m ....

6. 500 dm ....

7. 5,000 dm ....

Apply

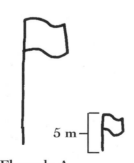

5 m —

Flagpole A   **Flagpole B**   **Flagpole C**

Estimate the height of these flagpoles.

  8. Flagpole A
  9. Flagpole B
  10. Flagpole C

When might you use estimating to solve a problem?
....
....
....

© GREAT SOURCE. ALL RIGHTS RESERVED.

 **Plan**

After your preview, make a plan. Choose a reading strategy that can help you meet your purpose.

> • **Use the strategy of visualizing and thinking aloud with math texts. It can make the questions and problems easier to solve.**

When you visualize, you make a mental picture of a problem. When you think aloud, you talk your way through a problem step by step.

During Reading

D Read with a Purpose

Now go back and do a careful reading of the chapter. Make notes on the stickies.

Using the Strategy

Directions: On the lines below, write a Think Aloud that explains how you would use estimating to solve the flagpole problem.

Think Aloud

....

....

....

....

....

....

....

....

© GREAT SOURCE. ALL RIGHTS RESERVED.

Understanding How Math Textbooks Are Organized

Thumb through your math text. You may notice that some or all of the chapters open with a study guide or "Goals" box. For example: ·············▶

After you read a math chapter, return to the Study Guide box. Check to see that you've met the goals and learned the definitions for each key term.

Directions: Answer these Study Guide questions. If you need help, look at the sticky notes you made while reading.

Goals

Learn to measure the length of an object in centimeters and decimeters. Estimate the length or width of an object in meters and kilometers.

Key Terms

centimeter
decimeter
meter
estimate
kilometer

1. What are centimeters, decimeters, meters, and kilometers? ....

....

2. How big is a decimeter? ....

....

3. How big is a meter? ....

....

4. How big is a kilometer? ....

....

5. Why might you use estimating to solve a metric measurement problem? ....

....

....

© GREAT SOURCE. ALL RIGHTS RESERVED.

E Connect

Making a connection to a math problem can help you solve it.

• Ask yourself, "What does this have to do with me?"

Directions: Estimate your height in centimeters. Then rewrite the measurement in decimeters and meters.

Measurement Chart

My height	
in centimeters	
in decimeters	
in meters	

After Reading

Each time you finish a chapter in your math book, take a few moments to reflect on what you've learned.

F Pause and Reflect

Think about your original reading purpose. Did you find out what you needed to know?

• At this point, ask yourself, "Did I meet my purpose?"

Directions: Return to the K-W-L Chart on page 44. Write what you learned about metric measurement in the L column. Then answer the question below.

What else do you need to know about this subject?

....

....

....

....

....

© GREAT SOURCE. ALL RIGHTS RESERVED.

Reread

Most students need to read a math chapter at least twice before they really *know* the material. If this is true for you, choose a strategy that can help you get more from your rereading.

• Use the strategy of note-taking when you reread.

Directions: Read the key words and topics in the left column. Make notes about them in the right column.

Key Word or Topic Notes

Key Words or Topics	My Notes
metric measurement	
metric units of length	
decimeter	
meter	
kilometer	
reading strategy	

Remember

You probably shouldn't close your math text until you're sure you remember what you've just learned.

• Creating sample tests can help you remember math material.

Directions: Make a sample math test. Write three problems that will test a classmate's understanding of metric units for length and width.

Sample Test

© GREAT SOURCE. ALL RIGHTS RESERVED.

NAME ....

FOR USE WITH PAGES 101–107

Focus on Word Problems

Most word problems are easier than they look. They become easier still if you use the reading process to solve them. Sharpen your skills here.

Step 1: Read.

Read every word problem twice or even three times—until you're sure you understand what the problem is asking for.

Directions: Read this word problem twice. Highlight key facts. Underline the main question.

> ### Sample Word Problem
>
> A school bus holds 62 children. How many school buses are needed to take 244 children, 6 teachers, and 9 parents on a field trip?

Step 2: Plan.

Next, choose your strategy. The strategy of visualizing and thinking aloud works well with word problems.

Directions: Make a sketch that reflects the problem.

Visualizing

© GREAT SOURCE. ALL RIGHTS RESERVED.

Textbooks

Step 3: Solve.

Use your Think Aloud and sketch to write the equation you'll use to solve the problem.

Directions: Write an equation for the field trip problem and then solve.

My equation

Step 4: Check.

Always check and double-check your work. Once again, the strategy of thinking aloud can help.

Directions: A good way to check for mistakes is to work backward. Write a Think Aloud that tells how you'd work backward to solve the field trip problem.

Think Aloud

© GREAT SOURCE. ALL RIGHTS RESERVED.

Focus on Questions

You'll find questions everywhere in your textbooks and tests. Since you can't get away from them, you might as well learn how to handle them. This plan can help.

Step 1: Read.

First, read the question over and over again, until you know what it is asking.

Directions: Read the two sample questions. Highlight key words.

> **Sample Fact Question**
>
> When did World War II begin and end?

> **Sample Critical Thinking Question**
>
> In what ways did World War II change the world?

Step 2: Think aloud.

Then use the strategy of thinking aloud to help you get a handle on how to answer the question.

Directions: Write a Think Aloud explaining what you need to do to answer the first question. Then do the same for the second question.

> **Think Aloud**

The factual question is asking me ....

....

The critical thinking question is asking me to ....

....

© GREAT SOURCE. ALL RIGHTS RESERVED.

Step 3: Gather information.

You'll find answers to factual questions in your textbook. To answer the critical thinking questions, combine information from the text with what you already know.

Directions: Explain where you will look for information for the two questions.

For question #1, I will ....

For question #2, I will ....

....

Step 4: Answer and check.

Use the information you've gathered to answer the questions.

Directions: Answer questions #1 and #2. Then exchange books with a partner, and "grade" his or her answer. Suggest improvements as needed.

My Answers

Question #1: ....

Question #2: ....

....

....

....

....

....

....

....

© GREAT SOURCE. ALL RIGHTS RESERVED.

Reading a Magazine Article ■

NAME .... FOR USE WITH PAGES 128–143

Reading a Magazine Article

You can use the reading process when you read a magazine article. The tools you've been reading about in the handbook will help you find the facts so you will understand the writer's message.

Before Reading

Here you'll practice using the reading process with a travel article about Niagara Falls.

A Set a Purpose

To set your purpose, ask a question about the topic of the article and why it's important.

- **Use key words from the title of the article to form a reading purpose question.**

Directions: Write your purpose for reading the magazine article "Niagara Falls: Wonder of the World." Then tell what you already know about the topic.

My purpose: ....

....

....

....

What I know about the topic: ....

....

....

....

© GREAT SOURCE. ALL RIGHTS RESERVED.

Nonfiction

B Preview

As always, your first step will be to preview the article. Look for clues about the topic of the article.

Directions: Preview the magazine article that follows. Write your preview notes on this chart.

Preview Chart

The title of the article is: ....

What I noticed about the art:	What I learned from the headings:

Niagara Falls

What I learned from the first and last paragraphs:	What I think the subject of this article is:

© GREAT SOURCE. ALL RIGHTS RESERVED.

KIDS TRAVEL! MAGAZINE ISSUE 27 FEBRUARY 21

Niagara Falls
WONDER OF THE WORLD

By Matthew Palatty

Niagara Falls is one of the most breathtaking places you'll ever visit. The sound of the rushing water, the sight of the whirling, swirling pools, the taste of the mist on your tongue—these are sensory experiences that you won't soon forget. They are also just a few of the reasons that Niagara Falls is one of the most popular tourist attractions in North America.

Off to the Mighty Falls

So let's say you and your family have decided to journey to Niagara Falls. To get the most out of your trip, you'll want to do a little planning beforehand. First, you'll need to learn where the falls are located and when they were formed.

Next, you'll want to figure out how to get to the falls and what you'll see once you arrive. But most

Did you know that one of the most amazing places on earth is here in North America—maybe right in your own backyard?

important, you'll want to find an answer to the question that has puzzled people for centuries: Why does all that water go rushing over that steep cliff day after day, year after year, century after century, without ever stopping? The answer to this question may be the most important item you bring with you on your trip to Niagara Falls.

Stop and Question

Why do you think the author asks you to imagine your own trip to Niagara Falls? (Write your answer on page 61.)

© GREAT SOURCE. ALL RIGHTS RESERVED.

Nonfiction

"Niagara Falls: Wonder of the World," continued

How the Falls Were Formed

Before you begin packing, learn a little about how the falls were formed. You probably already know that at one time, gigantic blocks of ice, called glaciers, covered the earth. These glaciers were very thick and very heavy. As they moved, they made huge ruts and holes in the surface of the earth. Some of these ruts and holes filled with water and became rivers and lakes. Others stayed dry and were valleys.

For thousands of years, the glaciers moved back and forth over the earth's surface. Then, toward the end of this Ice Age, a retreating glacier carved a sort of long cliff—called an escarpment—into the earth. Eventually, the waters of Lake Erie began flowing over the side of the escarpment and into Lake Ontario. The mighty Niagara Falls were formed.

Early History of the Falls

The first settlers at Niagara Falls were Native American men and women who came in search of good hunting ground. What they found pleased them to no end. The deep forests were filled with game and edible plants. The rivers and tributaries were well stocked with fish, and the winters were not overly harsh. Also, the falls themselves were an unending miracle—a sign that all was right in the world.

Stop and Question

Why does the author offer information about the history of Niagara Falls? (Write your answer on page 61.)

French Explorers Arrive

It wouldn't be long, however, before the peaceful lives of these Native Americans would end forever. In the late 1600s, white men made their way to the falls and claimed the area as their own. The earliest written description can be found in a book called *Nouvelle Découverte*, which was published in 1697 by a French man named Louis

© GREAT SOURCE. ALL RIGHTS RESERVED.

> "Niagara Falls: Wonder of the World," continued

Hennepin. Hennepin, who was part of a French expedition that was travelling through parts of North America, said that the falls reminded him of a tremendous wall of moving water.

Over the next hundred years, Niagara Falls attracted a great deal of attention. Several nations began fighting for control of the surrounding land. Native American tribes were forced out as various governments battled for "ownership" of the Niagara Falls region.

Today, the falls lie on the border between two countries: the United States and Canada. The falls have two principal parts, which are separated by Goat Island. The larger part, which is on the Canadian side, is called Horseshoe Falls. They are more than 185 feet high and approximately 2,700 feet long. On the right bank, New York State, are the American falls. Here the cliffs rise to a height of 190 feet and are 1,060 feet across. Both sides of the falls attract hundreds of thousands of visitors each year.

A Daredevil's Dream

It was during the 1800s that Niagara Falls became an important tourist attraction. People came by horse, boat, and train to marvel at the sight of the rushing water and experience the "curing powers" of the mist and fog.

Right from the beginning, there were some people who viewed the falls as a way to make big money. Daredevils built boats and bragged that they could "sail the falls"—for a price. Others stuffed themselves into barrels, boxes, and rubber balls and allowed themselves to be dropped over the falls. Very few of these daredevils survived the drop from the cliffs. Those that did were crushed by the weight of the water below.

Stop and Question

Why do you think the author chooses to include information about daredevils in this article? (Write your answer on page 61.)

The Unbelievable Blondin

For the most part, the daredevils who were smart enough to stay *away* from the water fared better. In fact, a couple managed to perform some amazing feats. The most notable of these daredevils was a French acrobat and tightrope walker named Blondin. In 1859, Blondin and his crew strung a 1,100-foot rope across the falls. Then, using only a pole for balance, the nimble Blondin tiptoed his way across the rope in under an hour's time.

In the years that followed, Blondin crossed and recrossed the

© GREAT SOURCE. ALL RIGHTS RESERVED.

"Niagara Falls: Wonder of the World," continued

falls several times. With each crossing, he managed to make the trip a bit more dangerous. Once, he crossed the falls with a blindfold on. Another time, he crossed with a man upon his back. On yet another trip, he stopped halfway across the tightrope and sat down to cook an omelet.

The Falls as We Know Them Today

If you visit the falls today, you won't see daredevils in barrels or tightrope walkers balancing chairs on their heads. But you *will* see nature at its finest and its fiercest. At certain times, the roar of the water is almost deafening. It's a booming, crashing sound very much like the sound of thunder during a violent spring storm. At other times, the mist from the falls is thick enough to block the view of the land at your feet. All you can see in front of you, behind you, and around you is rushing water. This is Niagara Falls, wonder of the world.

Stop and Question

How do you think the author feels about Niagara Falls? (Write your answer on page 61.)

C Plan

After you finish your preview, make a reading plan. Choose a strategy that can help you uncover the topic and most important ideas in the article.

• **You can use the strategy of questioning the author to get *more* from a magazine article.**

When you question the author, you think about decisions the author made when he or she was writing.

© GREAT SOURCE. ALL RIGHTS RESERVED.

During Reading

D Read with a Purpose

Now go back and do a careful reading of "Niagara Falls: Wonder of the World." Ask questions of the author as you read. Try to imagine how the author would respond to each question.

Directions: Write answers to your author questions here.

Questioning the Author

Page 57

Why do you think the author asks you to imagine your own trip to Niagara Falls?

Page 58

Why does the author offer information about the history of Niagara Falls?

Page 59

Why do you think the author chooses to include information about daredevils in

this article?

Page 60

How do you think the author feels about Niagara Falls?

© GREAT SOURCE. ALL RIGHTS RESERVED.

Using the Strategy

Questioning the author involves drawing conclusions about important facts and details in an article.

- **You can use a Double-entry Journal to record your thoughts and conclusions.**

Directions: Make notes about the Niagara Falls article on this Double-entry Journal.

Double-entry Journal

Text from the Article	My Thoughts and Feelings
"So let's say you and your family have decided to journey to Niagara Falls. To get the most out of your trip, you'll want to do a little planning beforehand."	
"It wouldn't be long, however, before the peaceful lives of these Native Americans would end forever."	
"Today, the falls lie on the border between two countries: the United States and Canada."	
"Once, he crossed the falls with a blindfold on. Another time, he crossed with a man upon his back. On yet another trip, he stopped halfway across the tightrope and sat down to cook an omelet."	

© GREAT SOURCE. ALL RIGHTS RESERVED.

Understanding How Magazine Articles Are Organized

Magazine articles are often organized around the 5 W's and H: *who, what, where, when, why,* and *how.* Looking for answers to these questions can strengthen your understanding of the article.

Directions: Complete this 5 W's and H Organizer with information from the Niagara Falls article.

5 W's and H Organizer

Subject: Niagara Falls

Who?

Where?

Why?

What?

How?

When?

E Connect with the Reading

Make a personal connection to the topic of a magazine article. This will make the article more interesting to read.

• **Recording your reactions can help you process and remember what you've learned.**

Directions: Complete these statements.

Here's how I felt as I read the article:

_____

_____

This is what I've learned:

_____

_____

© GREAT SOURCE. ALL RIGHTS RESERVED.

Nonfiction

After Reading

When reading, take a moment to reflect on your original purpose.

F Pause and Reflect

Keep in mind that your purpose was to find out about the topic and why it is important.

> • **Always ask yourself, "Did I meet my purpose for reading?"**

Directions: Check *yes* or *no* to the items on this list.

Purpose Checklist

	Yes	No
I have learned several important facts about Niagara Falls.		
I understand why the topic is important.		
I have evaluated the writer's evidence.		

G Reread

Remember that you can't believe everything you read. Always evaluate the information the writer presents.

> • **Use the strategy of reading critically to help you decide if the information in the article is reliable.**

© GREAT SOURCE. ALL RIGHTS RESERVED.

Directions: Answer these questions about the Niagara Falls article.

Critical Reading Chart

Questions	My Thoughts
Is the main idea or viewpoint clear?	
What evidence is presented?	
Is the evidence convincing?	
Is there another side to the story?	

Nonfiction

H Remember

Take what you learn from a magazine article and make it your own.

- **To remember a magazine article, connect what you've read to your own life.**

Directions: Use the Internet or the library to research a place you'd like to visit. List questions you have about the place on the lines below. Then use your research to help you answer them.

All about .... (Write the place you'd like to visit here.)

1. ....

Answer: ....

2. ....

Answer: ....

3. ....

Answer: ....

© GREAT SOURCE. ALL RIGHTS RESERVED.

Reading a News Story

A newspaper reporter's job is to give you the facts. Your job is to understand the facts and form opinions about what they mean.

Before Reading

The reading process can help you read a news story—whether for fun or for a class assignment.

A Set a Purpose

Your general purpose for reading a news story is to learn the facts and figure out what they mean.

- **To set your purpose, take several words from the headline and use them in a question.**

Directions: Write your purpose for reading the news story "Trucker Survives Deadly Attack by 'Killer' Bees." Then write some prereading questions about the article.

My purpose: ....

....

....

....

My prereading questions: ....

....

....

....

© GREAT SOURCE. ALL RIGHTS RESERVED.

 **Preview**

It's easy to preview a news story. Most of the facts you need appear in the first one or two paragraphs—the article's "lead."

Directions: Use this checklist to preview the truck driver article. Put a check mark next to each item after you look at it. Then answer the questions that follow.

◄ Preview Checklist

☐ Read the headline.

☐ Check the date.

☐ Skim the lead.

☐ Look for repeated words in the body of the article.

☐ Look at any photos or captions.

What is the story's headline?

....

Which newspaper published the story?

....

What is the name of the reporter?

....

What is the topic of the news story?

....

....

....

What did you learn from the lead?

....

....

....

What does this story or topic remind you of?

....

....

....

Nonfiction

© GREAT SOURCE. ALL RIGHTS RESERVED.

The Tampa Times

FINAL EDITION   MAY 10, 1992

Trucker Survives Deadly Attack by "Killer" Bees

BY AGNES SCOTTI

A Florida man last night lived through a midnight attack by an angry swarm of five million bees that were set free when the truck he was driving overturned in a deadly accident.

John Shane, 46, was stung by the insects after his truck was struck by an oncoming car. Shane, who was covered in countless shards of shattered glass, was trapped inside the twisted metal of his vehicle, which had been carrying 250 beehives to a local farmer.

Rescuers arrived on the scene within minutes of the collision. But their progress to free Shane was slow, partly because the bees stung them repeatedly as they cut their way into the cab of the truck.

Stop and Record

Who and what is the news story about? Make notes on your 5 W's and H Organizer (page 70).

Shortly after the accident occurred, the bees became agitated and swarmed the injured Shane, who said he began to feel "hot, pin-like jabs" to his face and neck.

Stop and Record

Where and when does the accident occur? Make notes on your 5 W's and H Organizer (page 70).

© GREAT SOURCE. ALL RIGHTS RESERVED.

"Trucker Survives Deadly Attack by 'Killer' Bees," continued

Stinging bees release a scent that encourages others in the swarm to follow suit. Angry bees also can be stimulated by noise and light. The sirens and flashing lights of the rescue vehicles that responded to the wreck agitated them even further. "Very few people can survive more than 200 bee stings," a rescuer said. "We were all frightened for the truck driver's life."

As firefighters worked to free Shane, a local beekeeper arrived to offer advice. At his suggestion, all lights at the scene were extinguished and Shane's truck was sprayed with a stream of water. The water seemed to calm the frantic bees.

Stop and Record

What happens after the truck crashes? Why do the bees attack Shane? Make notes on your 5 W's and H Organizer (page 70).

Shane, however, was becoming increasingly more alarmed by the bees. "Bees were crawling in and out of both his ears," a witness

recalled. "I'm surprised the man lasted as long as he did."

After more than two hours of waiting, Shane convinced a fire department cutting crew to hand over its equipment. Eventually, he was able to cut through the steering wheel that had pinned him to his seat.

Some 196 minutes after the accident occurred, Shane was rushed to the emergency room at a local hospital.

The driver suffered from multiple bee stings in addition to cuts, bruises, and a few sprains. "We knew we had to get him out of the truck before dawn," the beekeeper recalled later. "The light of day would have made the swarm only angrier."

As Shane's ambulance pulled away from the scene of the accident, a faint glimmer of light played in the eastern sky. The truck driver was saved with only a few minutes to spare.

Stop and Record

How does the driver free himself? Make notes on your 5 W's and H Organizer (page 70).

C Plan

Now make a plan that will help you uncover the facts of the story.

• Use the strategy of summarizing when reading a newspaper.

© GREAT SOURCE. ALL RIGHTS RESERVED.

Directions: As you read the story, make notes on this 5 W's and H Organizer. An organizer like this can help you get a handle on the most important facts and ideas.

5 W's and H Organizer

Who?	What?	When?

Subject _____

Where?	Why?	How?

These are the questions you should ask yourself while reading a news story.

During Reading

D Read with a Purpose

Now read the news story on pages 68–69, and complete the 5 W's and H Organizer.

© GREAT SOURCE. ALL RIGHTS RESERVED.

NAME ....

Using the Strategy

All kinds of reading tools work well with the strategy of summarizing. Choose the one that you think will help you the most.

• Readers often use a Web to keep track of key facts and details.

Directions: Complete this Web using facts from "Trucker Survives Deadly Attack by 'Killer' Bees."

◀ **Web**

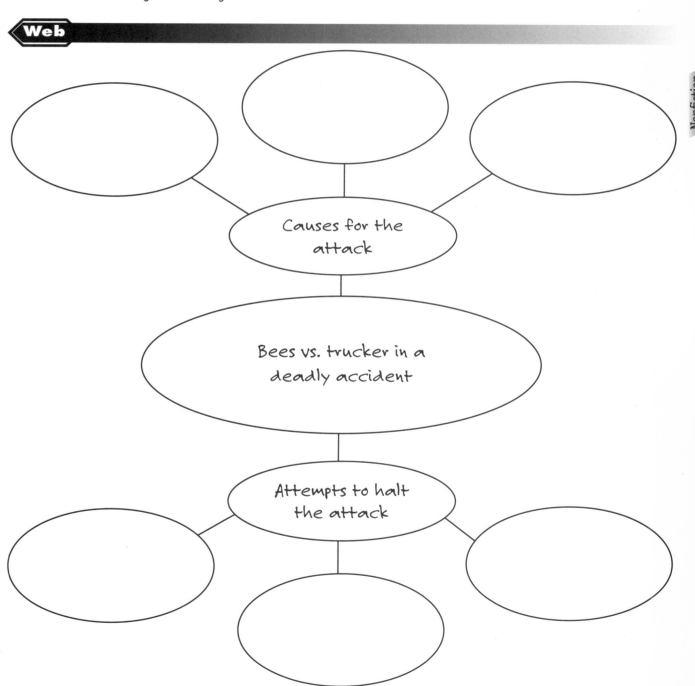

Causes for the attack

Bees vs. trucker in a deadly accident

Attempts to halt the attack

© GREAT SOURCE. ALL RIGHTS RESERVED.

Nonfiction

Understanding How Newspaper Articles Are Organized

In most news stories, the lead gives the most important information, including the main idea. The rest of the article *expands* on this information.

Think about the news story you just read. What would you say is the main idea? (Hint: Look at the headline and the first paragraph of the story.) Which details support the main idea?

Directions: Complete this Main Idea Organizer.

Main Idea Organizer

Main Idea		
Detail 1	Detail 2	Detail 3
Conclusion		

E Connect

The best way to make a connection to a news story is to imagine that you were there, witnessing the events as they unfolded.

• **Making a connection to a news story can strengthen your understanding of key facts and details.**

Directions: Write how you would have felt if you had been a witness to the bee attack.

I would have felt

because

© GREAT SOURCE. ALL RIGHTS RESERVED.

After Reading

Always spend a moment or more thinking about what you've learned from a news story.

F Pause and Reflect

At this point, decide whether or not you've met your reading purpose.

- **Ask yourself questions about your reading purpose and the news story itself.**

<u>Directions:</u> Complete this reading purpose checklist.

Purpose Checklist

Ask Yourself	Yes	No
Do I know the subject of the story?		
Do I know the main facts?		
Can I answer who, what, where, when, why, and how?		

G Reread

Some news stories require two careful readings. If you're not sure of every fact, you might want to spend some time rereading.

- **The strategy of reading critically can help you get *more* from your second reading.**

Reading critically means looking beyond the facts and details presented. It is reading "between the lines."

© GREAT SOURCE. ALL RIGHTS RESERVED.

Directions: Reread the truck article. Then make notes on this chart.

Critical Reading Chart

Questions	My Evaluation
1. Is the main idea or viewpoint clear?	
2. Is there evidence to support the main idea?	
3. Do the sources seem trustworthy?	
4. Is there another side to this story?	

H Remember

If you want to remember a news story, try telling someone about it.

• **To remember a news story, summarize it.**

Directions: In a brief email to a friend, describe the truck accident.

Email

....

....

....

....

....

....

....

© GREAT SOURCE. ALL RIGHTS RESERVED.

NAME ....

FOR USE WITH PAGES 157–166

Focus on Personal Essays

In a personal essay, a writer tells a story about an important experience. Your job is to understand the events of the experience and what they mean to the writer. This plan can help.

Step 1: Find the topic.

The topic of an essay is what the author is talking about.

Directions: Preview "On a Spring Saturday." Make notes on the stickies.

"On a Spring Saturday" by Luz Echeverria

Everything that happened was my fault. I know that. But sometimes I wonder if just a teeny amount of blame should go to my teacher. After all, it was his assignment that got me into this mess. So I kind of hint that I wouldn't mind if he takes some of the blame off of my aching shoulders and he tells me to forget it. I guess I figured he would say that.

But let me back up and explain myself. I'm a fifth grader at Tyler Park Elementary. I'm a pretty good student, and I've never been in any real trouble—until this spring, when I started my volunteering assignment.

Here's what happened. Every spring, all the fifth graders at Tyler have to spend a full Saturday volunteering somewhere. It's sort of a graduation requirement, I guess. Most kids volunteer in their neighborhoods. They baby-sit, clean houses, pick up trash, and stuff like that.

But I wanted to do something different—something no one had ever done before. So I said to my teacher, "I want to do something different, something no one has ever done before." He said that was fine. Then he told me that he would make arrangements for me to volunteer at the Maple Glen Retirement Home.

I figured this was a pretty good idea. First of all, I would be spending my Saturdays indoors. There would be no raking leaves in the freezing rain for me. Also, it would give me the chance to spend some time with my

© GREAT SOURCE. ALL RIGHTS RESERVED.

"On a Spring Saturday," continued

grandmother, who lives at Maple Glen. I figured I could sit with her for most of the day and maybe even watch a little TV. It would be a piece of cake.

So I told Mr. Sacks I liked the idea. He said that I should go to Maple Glen next Saturday and report to the head of volunteers. I said, "Piece of cake!"

But when Saturday arrived, I had a hard time getting out of bed, and I ended up being a little late. By the time I met up with Mrs. Williams, the head of volunteers, it was 9:30. Mrs. Williams looked sort of mad when she saw how late I was, but what was she going to do? So she gave me my assignment sheet for the day and told me to get cracking.

I was kind of surprised when I saw my assignment. I was supposed to go to the patients' living room and keep an eye on things there—for the whole day! Talk about boring. It sounded like I was going to sit around all day and do absolutely nothing. I could have done that at home!

But there was no point in complaining, and there was no one to complain to anyway. So I went to the patients' living room and took a quick look around. The room was empty except for one old lady who was just sitting there, staring at the TV. Talk about dull! So I gave the lady a friendly wave and kept going. I wanted to make it to my grandmother's room before breakfast was served!

It turns out I was right in time for breakfast. I enjoyed the food so much that I stayed for lunch, too. Actually, I pretty much spent the whole day in my grandmother's room. She slept a lot of the time, so I watched TV. A couple of times my grandmother asked me if I was supposed to be somewhere, but I told her that I had everything under control.

Only it turns out that I didn't. At the end of the day, I went back to the head of volunteers to have my card signed, and boy was she steamed! She told me that a lot of the guests had to spend the day alone because of me. She said that they go to the living room because they want someone to talk to. She said that they look forward to the Saturday visits from the volunteers. But today, thanks to me, there was no one there. So a lot of the guests got really upset and complained to Mrs. Williams.

At this point, I started to feel pretty bad. I tried to explain about my grandmother, but Mrs. Williams said that I could have brought her with me to the living room to spend the day. She said it would have been good for my grandmother, too. I told her I never thought of that, and she said it seemed like I hadn't thought about much besides myself. So I went home feeling really awful.

© GREAT SOURCE. ALL RIGHTS RESERVED.

"On a Spring Saturday," continued

On Monday, I told Mr. Sacks what happened. He told me that volunteering for a job is a serious responsibility. He reminded me that if you say you're going to do something, you have to do it, because people are counting on you. Then he suggested that I give it another try.

So that's why I'm here at Maple Glen on a sunny Saturday in June. I volunteer at Maple Glen three times a month now. Mostly I help out in the kitchen. Mrs. Williams says that pretty soon she'll trust me enough to assign me to the living room again. But first she needs to be sure that I'll put the guests' needs in front of my own.

I don't argue with her, of course, because I know she's right. I blew it my first time here. I didn't take the job seriously. But I've learned my lesson. Now I do the work I've been assigned, and I say thank you for the assignment. This is what I tell people when they ask me how I spend my time on Saturdays.

Here's what I noticed on my preview:

I found these repeated words:

I think the topic of the essay is:

Step 2: Find the main idea.

Next, draw conclusions about the main idea. Remember that the main idea is what the author has to say about the topic.

Finding the Main Idea

Subject + What the author says about the subject = The main idea.

Directions: Find the main idea in "On a Spring Saturday."

+

(Topic)   (What the author says about it)

=

(The main idea)

© GREAT SOURCE. ALL RIGHTS RESERVED.

FOR USE WITH PAGES 157–166

Step 3: Organize your thoughts.

Create an organizer that can help you see how the facts and details in the essay relate to the author's main idea.

Directions: Complete this Main Idea Organizer. First write the main idea. Then write three details that support the main idea.

Main Idea Organizer

Main Idea		
Detail 1	**Detail 2**	**Detail 3**

Step 4: Evaluate the main idea.

Finish by responding to the main idea. Do you agree or disagree with what the author is saying? Have you had a similar experience or feeling?

Directions: Write a journal entry about "On a Spring Saturday."

Journal Entry

© GREAT SOURCE. ALL RIGHTS RESERVED.

Focus on Persuasive Writing

In persuasive writing, an author gives an opinion or argues for or against a certain idea. Your job is to understand and evaluate the argument the writer presents. This three-step plan can help.

Step 1: Find the topic.

Remember that the topic is *who* or *what* the piece of writing is about.

Directions: Read the title and the first two paragraphs of this editorial. Then make notes on the sticky.

LUNCH PERIOD CHANGE WORRIES STUDENTS

Preview

The topic is:

....

....

....

I know this because:

....

....

....

....

BY JOE SCARAMUZZI

Yesterday, Principal Jared Meckler announced that beginning this January, lunch period for all students at George Washington Elementary will be ten minutes shorter. This change will affect all students, kindergarten through fifth.

Principal Meckler said he made the decision to slash ten minutes from the lunch hour only after months of careful thought and consideration. Mr. Meckler's plan is to give the extra ten minutes to the homeroom period at the beginning of the day. He says teachers will use the time for school announcements, student conferences, class meetings, and so on.

Principal Meckler promises that this change is in the students' best interest. But is this really true? We barely have enough time to eat as it is! Doesn't Mr. Meckler understand that it's possible to

© GREAT SOURCE. ALL RIGHTS RESERVED.

get stuck in the hot lunch line for twenty minutes or more? The change in the lunch hour will leave some unlucky kids with only ten minutes to eat. Bolting down your food and rushing to line up before the bell rings is certainly not in anyone's best interest.

It's certainly true that we need more homeroom time at the beginning of school. We could use this time to catch up on missed assignments or look at notes for an upcoming test. But that extra time shouldn't be subtracted from our lunch period. After all, lunchtime is practically the only time of the day that we have to relax.

But there is an easy solution to this problem. Some students and teachers have suggested to Mr. Meckler that he subtract two minutes from each academic period. This would give him the extra ten minutes he wants, without adversely affecting teachers or students. It's an idea that is well worth thinking about.

Step 2: Find the viewpoint.

During your careful reading, keep an eye out for the viewpoint. This is the statement of belief that the author wants to explain or support.

Directions: Now do a careful reading of the whole editorial. Make notes on the lines.

The viewpoint is:

I know this because:

© GREAT SOURCE. ALL RIGHTS RESERVED.

Step 3: Analyze the support.

Good persuasive writers know that in order to convince readers, they must offer plenty of support for their argument.

Directions: Complete this Argument Chart. Write the viewpoint and support in the first two columns. Then write your opinion about the argument and the support.

Argument Chart

Author's Viewpoint	Support	My Opinion
	Detail #1	Why I agree or disagree with the viewpoint:
	Detail #2	
	Detail #3	
		How the argument makes me feel:

Write the author's viewpoint here.

List the support the writer gives here.

Write your response to the argument here.

© GREAT SOURCE. ALL RIGHTS RESERVED.

Focus on Biography

Most biographers have two purposes in mind when writing. First, they want to tell an interesting story about the events of a person's life. Next, they want to create a "portrait" of that person.

Step 1: Read for key events.

Directions: Read this biography of Molly Pitcher. Look for key events in Pitcher's life. Record them on the Story String that follows.

"Molly Pitcher" by Rachael Haggerty

Mary Hays McCauly (who is better known as Molly Pitcher) was born in Trenton, New Jersey, in 1754. When she was still young, Mary moved with her family to Carlisle, Pennsylvania. Later, she was hired out as a servant girl to a wealthy Carlisle family. One day, Mary met the town barber, William Hays. They were married when Mary turned sixteen.

In 1777, William Hays enlisted as a gunner in a Pennsylvania army regiment. It was decided that Mary would accompany him as he traveled with the regiment. At that time, it was common for a woman to go with her husband into battle.

On June 28, 1778, Mary watched from a distance as her husband and others fought a bloody battle at Monmouth Courthouse in New Jersey. The day was brutally hot—so much so that men were falling to the ground from the heat, rather than from any injuries.

Eager to help, Mary began running back and forth from the Monmouth town well to the regiment's front lines. In her hands she carried pitchers of water to cool the men and their cannons.

After the battle was over, word of Mary's bravery spread. People began saying that the battle of Monmouth would have been lost without the help of a woman named "Molly Pitcher." When General George Washington caught wind of what she had done, he dubbed her "Sergeant Molly." However, she is forever remembered as Molly Pitcher, the woman who saved many lives with just a simple pitcher of water.

© GREAT SOURCE. ALL RIGHTS RESERVED.

◀ **Story String**

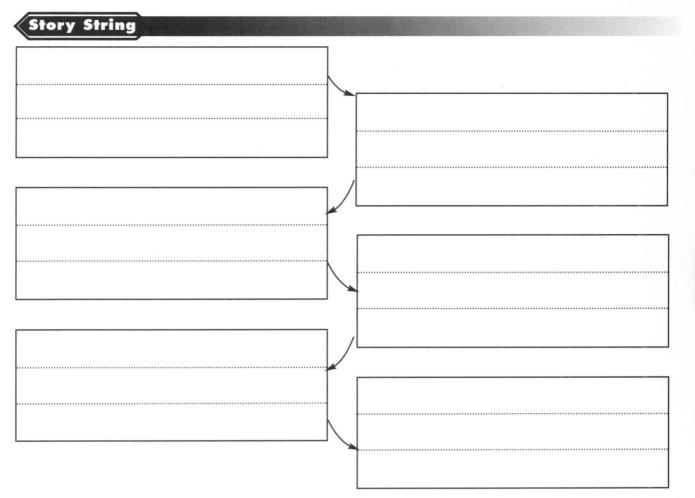

Nonfiction

Step 2: Form a portrait of the subject.

As you read, look for clues about the subject's personality. Try to see the "portrait" the writer is "painting."

Directions: Complete this Thinking Tree about Molly Pitcher. On the lines, write words that describe her. Then write "proof" for the words.

◀ **Thinking Tree**

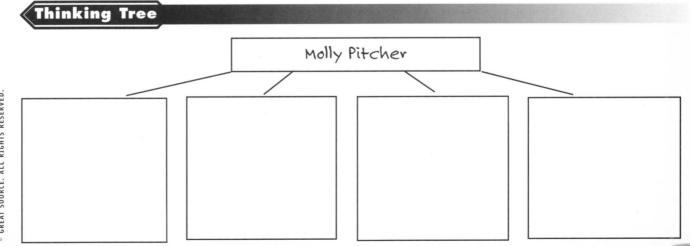

© GREAT SOURCE. ALL RIGHTS RESERVED.

Step 3: Discover cause and effect.

Next, put all the facts together, and think about how events and experiences shaped the person's personality.

Directions: Complete this Cause-Effect Organizer about Molly Pitcher.

◀ Cause-Effect Organizer

Effects

Cause

Mary delivers water to
the soldiers.

Step 4: Respond to the biographical subject.

It's important that you form your own impression of the biographical subject. Your opinion may or may not be the same as the biographer's opinion.

Directions: Write your opinion of Molly Pitcher. Then explain why you feel that way.

◀ Opinion Statement

© GREAT SOURCE. ALL RIGHTS RESERVED.

Nonfiction

Focus on Real-world Writing

Real-world writing is informational reading. It is bus schedules, directions for playing a game, and a recipe for your favorite dessert. Here is a plan that can help you get more from this type of reading.

Step 1: Know what you're after.

First, understand your purpose for reading. Ask yourself, "What do I need to know?"

Directions: Look at this notice about an upcoming book sale. Then write your reading purpose on the sticky.

JENKINTOWN ELEMENTARY BOOK SALE

Come one, come all to Jenkintown Elementary's annual book sale!
Everyone is welcome!

Featuring books for students in grades K–12

Date: Friday, March 4

Time: 9:00 A.M. to 3:00 P.M. and 6:00 P.M. to 8:00 P.M.

Location: Jenkintown Elementary School Cafeteria

Sponsor: Jenkintown Elementary PTO

Here is your chance to stock up on your favorite authors, including:

Judy Blume   Matt Christopher   Ann Martin   Gary Paulsen

Maurice Sendak   Lois Lowry   Walter Dean Myers   Richard Peck

and many, many more!

My purpose is

All book sale customers will be entered automatically in a drawing for a **free $50.00 gift certificate** to be used at Tesser and Sons Booksellers.

© GREAT SOURCE. ALL RIGHTS RESERVED.

Step 2: Figure out how the material is organized.

Preview to get a sense of how the material is organized.
Look for items on the checklist. Then write your notes.

Preview Checklist

☐ Main headings and titles

☐ Boldface and emphasized terms

☐ Lists or outlines

Directions: Preview the book sale flyer. Write what you noticed on the chart.

Preview Chart

Main headings and titles	Boldface and emphasized terms	Lists or outlines

© GREAT SOURCE. ALL RIGHTS RESERVED.

Step 3: Find out what you need to know.

Try to read only the information that is relevant to you. Pay attention only to what *you* need to know.

Directions: Read the flyer carefully. Use a highlighter to mark the most important information. Then make notes on this Web.

> **Web**

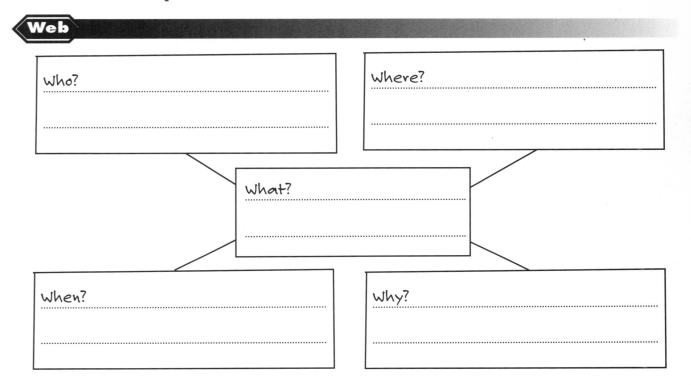

Who?

Where?

What?

When?

Why?

Step 4: Remember and use the information.

If you'll need the information later, make some notes and put your notes in a safe place.

Directions: Write information about the book sale on this calendar page.

Friday, March

4

Memo:

© GREAT SOURCE. ALL RIGHTS RESERVED.

Reading a Folktale

Folktales are stories that have been handed down from one generation to the next. Very often the purpose of a folktale is to teach a lesson. Your job is to read the tale and understand the lesson. In addition, you'll need to consider how the lesson relates to your own life. The reading process can help.

Before Reading

Watch for these literary elements as you read: setting, characters, plot, and theme.

A Set a Purpose

To set your purpose, ask yourself about the plot and lesson of the folktale.

- **Ask one question about the folktale and another question about the lesson it teaches.**

Directions: Write your purpose for reading the African folktale, "The Bravest of All Men." Then make a prediction about the story.

Purpose question #1:

....

....

Purpose question #2:

....

....

My prediction:

....

....

© GREAT SOURCE. ALL RIGHTS RESERVED.

NAME _____

FOR USE WITH PAGES 212–224

B Preview

Your next job is to preview the folktale. Review the checklist
on page 213 of your handbook. Write your notes on a Preview Chart.

Directions: Preview "The Bravest of All Men." Write your notes here.

Preview Chart

Preview Questions	My Notes
What is the title of the tale?	
Where does the story come from?	
What repeated words and names did you see?	
What did you learn from the first paragraph?	
What did you learn from the last paragraph?	

Fiction

© GREAT SOURCE. ALL RIGHTS RESERVED.

THE BRAVEST OF ALL MEN
AN AFRICAN FOLKTALE RETOLD BY DARRYL GREENWOOD

A proud and plucky man named Sedu lived in the African village of Golo. Sedu was a hunter, and believed himself to be the bravest of all men. Whenever the men of Golo went hunting, Sedu accompanied them. When the men returned, Sedu would say to his wife, "Among all the hunters, I was the bravest. Standing alone, I fought with the leopard. I alone chased the elephant. When I went forward with my spear, even the mighty lion fled. I am the most courageous of all hunters, and the bravest of all men."

His wife, Ladi, would always ask, "Did no one but you bring back meat?"

And Sedu would reply, "Yes, they have brought back meat. But this is thanks to my fearlessness. I brought luck to the others."

Once, when the people said that the enemy was near, Sedu and the other men of the village went into the bush country. When they returned, Sedu hung his spear on the wall and said to his wife, "When I ran toward the enemy, they turned and fled. My reputation grows larger each day. I am the bravest of all warriors. Not even the fiercest of our enemies dare cross me. What say you to this, wife?"

And Ladi answered, "It is so."

Stop and Record
Make some notes in boxes 1 and 2 of your Story String on page 93.

After many years of this, there was a funeral in a distant village. Many of the women of Golo wished to go. But the men were working the fields and could not accompany them. So Ladi told the women, "My husband is the bravest of all men. He will take us through the forest. With Sedu as our guide, we can walk without fear."

So Ladi approached her husband. "The women who are going to the funeral agree that you are the one to take them through the forest," she said to Sedu. "Will you take us?"

Sedu sighed and said, "From one day to the next, no one mentions my courage. It goes unnoticed. But when courage is needed, people ask, 'Where is Sedu?'"

"This is true, Sedu," Ladi replied. "But even so, will you take us?"

© GREAT SOURCE. ALL RIGHTS RESERVED.

"The Bravest of All Men," continued

"Of course, Ladi," Sedu replied. "I will guide you through the forest. How can I not? The women of Golo must be kept safe."

So Sedu took his spear and went into the forest with the women.

On this day, there were warriors of the enemy in the forest hunting game. When they saw Sedu leading the group of women, they laughed amongst themselves. "Look at how the man struts like a guinea fowl," they cackled. "Let us strike fear into him."

So they hid themselves near the trail. When Sedu and the women approached, the hunters came out of the brush and surrounded the women of Golo.

Sedu shouted, "We are surrounded! Run for the trees!"

The women and Sedu ran to the trees as quickly as they could and tried to hide themselves. But they were soon captured by the enemy warriors.

Stop and Record
Make some notes in boxes 3 and 4 of your Story String on page 93.

The warriors surrounded the women and Sedu, and one of the hunters said to Sedu's wife, "What is your name?"

And she replied, "Ladi."

"Ladi is a name used by the women of our tribe as well," the leader of the warriors said proudly. "Because you are called Ladi, we will not hurt you."

To another woman he said, "What is your name?"

Seeing how good it was to be named Ladi, the woman replied, "My name is also Ladi."

The leader of the warriors said, "A good name. We shall not hurt you."

He asked another woman and she too replied, "Ladi."

All of the women were asked, and all of them answered, "My name is Ladi."

Then the leader of the warriors turned to Sedu. "All of the women of your tribe are called Ladi. I think it a strange custom. In our tribe, every woman has her own name. But you, guinea fowl who leads the guinea hens, what are you called?"

"I," said Sedu, "I too am called Ladi."

When the warriors heard this, they laughed with glee. "No," declared the leader, "it is not possible. Ladi is a woman's name. You are a man with a spear. Are you telling me that the men of your village are *also* called Ladi?"

© GREAT SOURCE. ALL RIGHTS RESERVED.

Fiction

"No, no," replied Sedu nervously. "Only the women are called Ladi."

"As it should be," the leader replied. "But then why are you called Ladi?"

Sedu looked around him, back and forth, behind him and in front, but he saw no chance of escape. "You see," he said slowly, "appearances are deceiving. I too am a woman."

With this the enemy roared in laughter. The women of Golo laughed too. In fact, everyone laughed but Sedu.

Stop and Record
Make some notes in boxes 5 and 6 of your Story String on page 93.

Then Sedu's wife spoke. "He speaks modestly of himself. This is the courageous Sedu, the famous Sedu."

Sedu nodded his head with reluctance. "Yes, it is so. I am Sedu. The woman speaks the truth."

So the leader said, "People say that Sedu claims to be the bravest of all men."

"No," Sedu replied, "this is no longer so. I *used* to be the bravest of all men, you see. But now I am only the bravest in my village."

The hunters laughed some more, and then let the group go. Sedu and the women went to the funeral, and afterward returned to Golo.

Upon their return, everyone was laughing at Sedu. Instead of calling him by his name, they called him Ladi. So Sedu went into his house and shut the door. Whenever he came out, however, the people of Golo laughed. Sedu could not hide from the shame.

At last, Sedu sent his wife to tell them this: "Sedu, who was formerly the bravest of men, was reduced to being the bravest of his village. But from now on, he is not the bravest in the village. He claims to be only as brave as other people."

With this, the people of Golo stopped making fun of Sedu. And thereafter, he was no braver than anyone else.

Stop and Record
Make some notes in boxes 7 and 8 of your Story String on page 93.

© GREAT SOURCE. ALL RIGHTS RESERVED.

C Plan

Next, make a plan. Choose a strategy that can help you understand the folktale and its lesson.

- **The strategy of using graphic organizers works well with folktales.**

A Story String is a graphic organizer that can help you keep track of key events in a plot.

During Reading

D Read with a Purpose

Once you've decided on a strategy, you're ready to do a careful reading of the selection.

Directions: Make notes on this organizer as you read "The Bravest of All Men."

Story String

1.

2.

3.

4.

5.

6.

7.

8.

© GREAT SOURCE. ALL RIGHTS RESERVED.

Fiction

Using the Strategy

All kinds of graphic organizers work with folktales. Choose the one that can help you the most.

- **A Story Organizer simplifies a story and makes it easier to understand what happens.**

Directions: Summarize what happens in "The Bravest of All Men" on this Story Organizer.

Story Organizer

Beginning

▼

Middle

▼

End

© GREAT SOURCE. ALL RIGHTS RESERVED.

Understanding How Folktales Are Organized

While it's true that every folktale is different, most follow a similar pattern.

Directions: Reread page 220 in your handbook. Then complete this Plot Diagram for "The Bravest of All Men."

Plot Diagram

"The Bravest of All Men"

4. Climax (Action reaches a critical point):

3. Rising action (How the characters try to solve the problem):

2. Conflict (The problem the characters face):

1. Opening event (What happens first):

5. Resolution (How things turn out):

© GREAT SOURCE. ALL RIGHTS RESERVED.

Fiction

E **Connect**

As you read, keep track of the personal connections you make to a folktale. Ask yourself, "How do I feel about the characters? Has something similar happened to me or someone I know?"

- **Making connections to a folktale can help you better understand its lesson.**

<u>Directions:</u> Explain your connections to the folktale you just read.

Making Connections

Connection Questions	My Answer
Which of the characters did you find most interesting?	
In what ways does this character remind you of yourself or someone you know?	
How did you feel about the plot of the tale as you were reading?	
What event in your own life does the folktale remind you of?	

© GREAT SOURCE. ALL RIGHTS RESERVED.

NAME ....

FOR USE WITH PAGES 212–224

After Reading

When you finish a folktale, take a moment to consider what you've learned. This will help you better understand and remember the story.

F Pause and Reflect

Think again about your purpose. Recall the questions you asked yourself before reading the folktale.

• **When you reflect, ask yourself, "Do I know what the folktale is about? Do I understand the lesson to be learned?"**

Directions: Circle the answers that apply to you. Then explain your answers.

I know what the folktale is about.   I don't know what the folktale is about.

I understand the folktale's lesson.   I don't understand the folktale's lesson.

Here's why: ....

....

....

G Reread

Very often you can find answers to your questions by rereading some or all of the folktale. Think about the major literary elements as you reread:

   ☐ Setting

   ☐ Character

   ☐ Plot

   ☐ Theme

• **Use the rereading strategy of close reading.**

Fiction

© GREAT SOURCE. ALL RIGHTS RESERVED.

Directions: Look at these lines from the folktale. Then write your thoughts and feelings.

Double-entry Journal

Lines from the folktale	What it means or how it makes me feel
"When I ran toward the enemy, they turned and fled. My reputation grows larger each day. I am the bravest of all warriors."	
"Sedu looked around him, back and forth, behind him and in front, but he saw no chance of escape. "You see," he said slowly, "appearances are deceiving. I too am a woman."	
"Sedu, who was formerly the bravest of men, was reduced to being the bravest of his village. But from now on, he is not the bravest in the village. He claims to be only as brave as other people."	

H Remember

You can remember a folktale by thinking of it in modern terms.

• **Make a folktale your own by "updating" it.**

Directions: Turn "The Bravest of All Men" into a modern-day story. Write the first paragraph of your story on the lines below.

Journal Entry

....

....

....

© GREAT SOURCE. ALL RIGHTS RESERVED.

Reading a Novel

Reading a novel is a little like taking an adventure. There are new people to meet and new places to see. Think of the reading process as a guidebook to use along the way. It can help you get more from your reading adventure.

Before Reading

There's a lot to keep track of when you're reading a novel. You have to get to know the characters, become familiar with the setting, and understand what's happening in the plot. The reading process can help. Begin by setting your purpose.

A Set a Purpose

Your primary purpose when reading a novel is to enjoy it. But you can't enjoy something if you don't understand it. So, *understanding* the novel is also an important reading purpose.

- **To set your purpose, ask and answer important questions about three major elements of the novel: characters, setting, and plot.**

Directions: You will be reading a part of the classic novel *The Call of the Wild*. What should be your purpose for reading? Write three questions below. (We've done the first one for you.)

◄ Purpose Chart

Element	My Questions
characters	Who are the most important characters?
setting	
plot	

© GREAT SOURCE. ALL RIGHTS RESERVED.

Fiction

B Preview

Previewing a novel is as easy as looking at the front and back covers and thumbing through the pages.

Directions: Preview the front and back covers of *The Call of the Wild*. Make notes on the sticky notes.

Back Cover

This classic story of survival, which was first published in 1903, is widely regarded as Jack London's masterwork.

❀ ❀ ❀

The Call of the Wild is the story of a courageous dog named Buck, who is kidnapped from his master and sent to the Klondike gold fields in Alaska to become a sled dog. In his struggle for survival, Buck learns some valuable lessons about the unbreakable bonds between man, dog, and wilderness. Even more important, he learns what it means to love life and listen to the call of the wild.

"One of the finest children's books of all time."

—*Teacher's Press* Magazine

Front Cover

Classics Books Presents . . .

The *Call of the* *Wild*

by Jack London

The title:
....
....
....

The author:
....
....

Important information about the author:
....
....
....

Important information about the book:
....
....
....

The book review tells me:
....
....
....

© GREAT SOURCE. ALL RIGHTS RESERVED.

C Plan

Choose a reading strategy that can help you explore important literary elements in the novel. Good readers often use the strategy of synthesizing.

• **Synthesizing means looking at different elements of the novel—characters, setting, and plot—and seeing how they work together.**

Directions: Make notes on this Fiction Organizer as you read the excerpt from *The Call of the Wild*.

Fiction Organizer

Characters Who are they?

What are they like?

Setting Where does the novel take place?

When does it take place?

Title
The Call of the Wild

Plot What happens?

© GREAT SOURCE. ALL RIGHTS RESERVED.

Fiction

During Reading

D Read with a Purpose

Now read this part of *The Call of the Wild*. As you read, think about the characters, setting, and plot.

Directions: Underline clues about characters, setting, and plot as you read. Make notes on your Fiction Organizer.

from *The Call of the Wild* by Jack London

For two days and nights the baggage car that was Buck's prison was dragged along at the tail of a shrieking locomotive; and for two days and nights Buck neither ate nor drank. In his anger, he had met the first advances of the baggage handlers with growls, and they had retaliated by teasing him. When he flung himself against the bars of his cage, quivering and frothing, they laughed at him and taunted him. They growled and barked like detestable dogs, mewed, and flapped their arms and crowed. It was all very silly, he knew; but therefore the more outrage to his dignity, and his anger grew and grew. He did not mind the hunger so much, but the lack of water caused him severe suffering and fanned his wrath to fever-pitch. Even worse, the ill treatment had flung him into a fever, which was fed by the inflammation of his parched and swollen throat and tongue.

He was glad for one thing—the rope was off his neck. That had given them an unfair advantage; but now that it was off, he would show them. They would never get another rope around his neck. That was a promise he made to himself.

For two days and nights Buck neither ate nor drank, and during those two days and nights of torment, he accumulated a fund of wrath that boded ill for whoever first fell foul of him. His eyes turned blood-shot, and he was metamorphosed into a raging fiend. So changed was he that the Judge himself would not have recognized him; and the baggage handlers breathed a sigh of relief when they bundled him off the train at Seattle.

Stop and Record

Make some notes in the "Setting" section of the Fiction Organizer on page 101.

Four men gingerly carried the crate from the wagon into a small, high-walled back yard. A stout man, with a red sweater that sagged generously

© GREAT SOURCE. ALL RIGHTS RESERVED.

NAME

from _The Call of the Wild_, continued

at the neck, came out and signed the book for the driver. This man, Buck knew, would be his next tormentor, so he hurled himself savagely against the bars. The man smiled grimly, and brought a hatchet and a club.

"You ain't going to take him out now?" the driver asked.

"Sure," the man replied, driving the hatchet into the crate for a pry.

There was an instantaneous scattering of the four men who had carried the crate in, and from safe perches on top the wall they prepared to watch the performance.

Buck rushed at the splintering wood, sinking his teeth into it, surging and wrestling with it. Wherever the hatchet fell on the outside, he was there on the inside, snarling and growling, as furiously anxious to get out as the man in the red sweater was calmly intent on getting him out.

"Now, you red-eyed devil," he said, when he had made an opening sufficient for the passage of Buck's body. At the same time he dropped the hatchet and shifted the club to his right hand.

And Buck was truly a red-eyed devil, as he drew himself together for the spring, hair bristling, mouth foaming, a mad glitter in his blood-shot eyes. Straight at the man he launched his one hundred and forty pounds of fury. In mid air, just as his jaws were about to close on the man, he received a shock that checked his body and brought his teeth together with an agonizing clip. He whirled over, fetching the ground on his back and side. He had never been struck by a club in his life, and did not understand. With a snarl that was part bark and more scream, he was again on his feet and launched into the air. And again the shock came and he was brought crushingly to the ground. This time he was aware that it was the club, but his madness knew no caution. A dozen times he charged, and just as often the club broke the charge and smashed him down.

Stop and Record

Make some notes about Buck in the "Characters" section of the Fiction Organizer on page 101.

After a particularly fierce blow, he crawled to his feet, too dazed to rush. He staggered limply about, the blood flowing from nose and mouth and ears, his beautiful coat sprayed and flecked with bloody slaver. Then the man advanced and deliberately dealt him a frightful blow on the nose. All the pain he had endured was as nothing compared with the exquisite agony

© GREAT SOURCE. ALL RIGHTS RESERVED.

from *The Call of the Wild,* continued

of this. With a roar that was almost lionlike in its ferocity, he again hurled himself at the man. But the man, shifting the club from right to left, coolly caught him by the under jaw, at the same time wrenching downward and backward. Buck turned a complete circle in the air, and half of another, then crashed to the ground on his head and chest.

For the last time he rushed. The man struck the shrewd blow he had purposely withheld for so long, and Buck crumpled up and went down, knocked utterly senseless.

Stop and Record

Make some notes about the man in the red sweater in the "Characters" section of the Fiction Organizer on page 101.

"He's no slouch at dog-breakin', that's wot I say," one of the men on the wall cried enthusiastically.

"Druther break cayuses any day, and twice on Sundays," was the reply of the driver, as he climbed on the wagon and started the horses.

Buck's senses came back to him, but not his strength. He lay where he had fallen, and from there he watched the man in the red sweater.

"'Answers to the name of Buck,'" the man soliloquized, quoting from the saloon-keeper's letter which had announced the consignment of the crate and contents. "Well, Buck, my boy," he went on in a genial voice, "we've had our little ruction, and the best thing we can do is to let it go at that. You've learned your place, and I know mine. Be a good dog and all 'll go well and the goose hang high. Be a bad dog, and I'll whale the stuffin' outa you. Understand?"

As he spoke he fearlessly patted the head he had so mercilessly pounded, and though Buck's hair involuntarily bristled at touch of the hand, he endured it without protest. When the man brought him water he drank eagerly, and later bolted a generous meal of raw meat, chunk by chunk, from the man's hand.

He was beaten (he knew that); but he was not broken. He saw, once for all, that he stood no chance against a man with a club. He had learned the lesson, and in all his after life he never forgot it.

Stop and Record

Now make notes in the "Plot" section of the Fiction Organizer on page 101.

© GREAT SOURCE. ALL RIGHTS RESERVED.

Using the Strategy

You can use the strategy of synthesizing to zero in on a single literary element. For example, you might use the strategy to explore the characters in a work.

• **Use the strategy of synthesizing to help you focus on a single literary element.**

Directions: Write your notes about Buck on the first Character Map. Write your notes about the man in the red sweater on the second.

Character Map

What the character says and does	How the character looks and feels

BUCK

What others think about the character	How I feel about the character

© GREAT SOURCE. ALL RIGHTS RESERVED.

Fiction

Character Map

What the character says and does
....
....
....
....
....
....
....

How the character looks and feels
....
....
....
....
....
....
....

Man in the red sweater

What Others think about the character
....
....
....
....
....

How I feel about the character
....
....
....
....
....

Understanding How Novels Are Organized

The plot of a novel is just as important as the characters. Careful readers keep track of the individual events that make up the plot. Once again, the strategy of synthesizing can help.

- **You can use a Story String to show the sequence of events in a plot.**

© GREAT SOURCE. ALL RIGHTS RESERVED.

Directions: Use this Story String to show what happens in this part of *The Call of the Wild*.

Story String

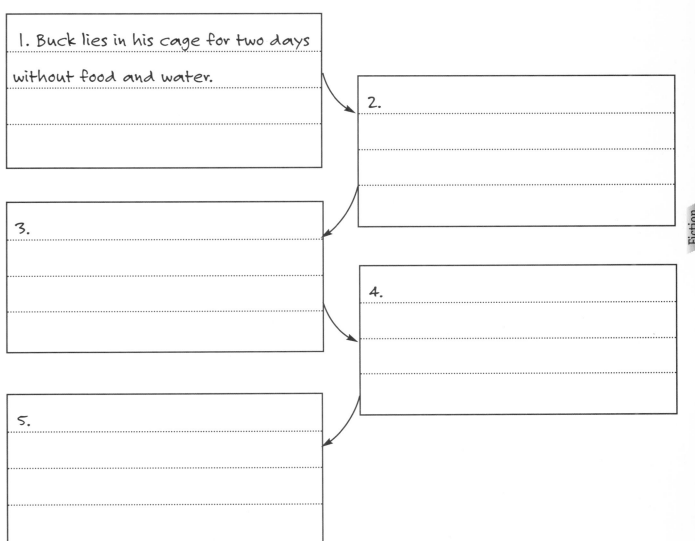

1. Buck lies in his cage for two days without food and water.

2.

3.

4.

5.

E Connect

As you read, ask yourself, "What is my reaction to the characters and the events of the story? How would I act if the same thing happened to me?" Questions like these can help you feel involved in what you're reading.

• **Good readers make connections between the novel and their own lives.**

© GREAT SOURCE. ALL RIGHTS RESERVED.

Fiction

Directions: Read the quotes in the left-hand column of the Double-entry Journal. In the right-hand column, tell how they make you feel.

Double-entry Journal

Quotes	My thoughts and reactions
"When he flung himself against the bars of his cage, quivering and frothing, they laughed at him and taunted him."	
"They would never get another rope around his neck. That was a promise he made to himself."	
"In mid air, just as his jaws were about to close on the man, he received a shock that checked his body and brought his teeth together with an agonizing clip."	
"For the last time he rushed. The man struck the shrewd blow he had purposely withheld for so long, and Buck crumpled up and went down, knocked utterly senseless."	
"He was beaten (he knew that); but he was not broken."	

© GREAT SOURCE. ALL RIGHTS RESERVED.

After Reading

After you finish a novel, spend time thinking about some of its "big ideas." Pull all of its individual parts together—the characters, setting, and plot. This can help you figure out the author's theme.

F Pause and Reflect

Think back on what you've read.

• **Ask yourself, "How well did I meet my purpose?"**

Directions: If you feel you understand how the element works in this part of *The Call of the Wild,* put a √ in Column 2. If you need to think some more about the element, put a √ in Column 3.

Checklist

Element	I understand it very well.	I need to understand it better.
characters		
setting		
plot		
theme		

G Reread

If you're not sure how an element works in a novel, you'll need to do some rereading.

• **Use the strategy of graphic organizers to help you explore a major element, such as theme.**

Directions: Review the notes you've made about *The Call of the Wild.* Then complete this Theme Diagram.

© GREAT SOURCE. ALL RIGHTS RESERVED.

Theme Diagram

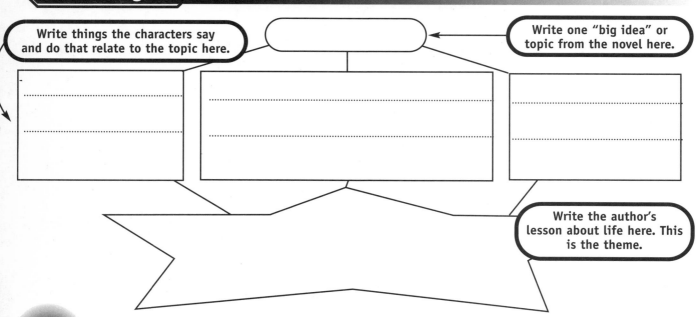

Write things the characters say and do that relate to the topic here.

Write one "big idea" or topic from the novel here.

Write the author's lesson about life here. This is the theme.

H Remember

Good readers remember what they've read.

• **To help you remember a novel, give it a rating and then explain your opinion.**

Directions: Rate the selection from *The Call of the Wild*. Then tell why you would or would not like to read more of the novel.

Characters

1	2	3	4	5	6	7	8	9	10
Believable			Somewhat Believable				Very Believable		

Setting

1	2	3	4	5	6	7	8	9	10
Developed			Somewhat Developed				Well Developed		

Plot

1	2	3	4	5	6	7	8	9	10
Dull			Interesting				Very Interesting		

Why I would or would not want to read more of this novel:

© GREAT SOURCE. ALL RIGHTS RESERVED.

Focus on (Characters)

In some stories, it's the characters you remember most. You admire them, you fear for them, you laugh with them or at them. Here's a plan to help you focus on a central character in a story, novel, or play.

Step 1: "Listen" to and "watch" the character.

"Listen" to what the character says and "watch" what he or she does.

Directions: Read this excerpt from the novel *Joey Pigza Swallowed the Key*. Highlight everything Joey *says*. Underline what he *does*.

from *Joey Pigza Swallowed the Key* by Jack Gantos

At school they say I'm wired bad, or wired mad, or wired sad, or wired glad, depending on my mood and what teacher has ended up with me. But there is no doubt about it. I'm *wired*.

This year was no different. When I started out all the days there looked about the same. In the morning I'd be okay and follow along in class. But after lunch, when my meds had worn down, it was nothing but trouble for me.

One day, we were doing math drills in class and every time Mrs. Maxy asked a question, like "What's nine times nine?" I'd raise my hand because I'm really quick at math. But each time she called on me, even though I knew the answer, I'd just blurt out, "Can I get back to you on that?" Then I'd nearly fall out of my chair from laughing. And she'd give me that white-lipped look which meant, "Settle down." But I didn't and kept raising my hand each time she asked a question until finally no other kid would raise their hand because they knew what was coming between me and Mrs. Maxy.

Step 2: Create a Character Map.

Next, think about how the character looks and acts.

© GREAT SOURCE. ALL RIGHTS RESERVED.

Fiction

Directions: Complete this Character Map about Joey.

Character Map

WHAT THE CHARACTER SAYS	WHAT THE CHARACTER DOES

Joey

HOW THE CHARACTER FEELS ABOUT OTHERS	HOW OTHERS FEEL ABOUT THE CHARACTER

Step 3: Make inferences about the character.

Now use your critical thinking skills to make some inferences about the character.

Directions: Write your inferences about Joey in Column 2.

Inference Chart

What the character does and says	My conclusions about the character

© GREAT SOURCE. ALL RIGHTS RESERVED.

Focus on Setting

Understanding a setting means knowing where and when a story takes place. It also means thinking about the effect the setting has on the characters and the overall feeling, or mood, of the story. Follow these steps.

Step 1: Read carefully.

Directions: Read this excerpt from the classic novel *Caddie Woodlawn*. Underline clues about time. Highlight clues about place.

from *Caddie Woodlawn* by Carol Ryrie Brink

In 1864 Caddie Woodlawn was eleven, and as wild a little tomboy as ever ran the woods of western Wisconsin. She was the despair of her mother and of her elder sister Clara. But her father watched her with a little shine of pride in his eyes, and her brothers accepted her as one of themselves without a question. Indeed, Tom, who was two years older, and Warren, who was two years younger than Caddie, needed Caddie to link them together into an inseparable trio. Together they got in and out of more scrapes and adventures than any one of them could have imagined alone. And in those pioneer days Wisconsin offered plenty of opportunities for adventure to three wide-eyed, red-headed youngsters.

On a bright Saturday afternoon in the early fall Tom and Caddie and Warren Woodlawn sat on a bank of the Menomonie River, or Red Cedar as they call it now, taking off their clothes. Their red heads shone in the sunlight. Tom's hair was the darkest, Caddie's the nearest golden, and nine-year-old Warren's was plain carrot color. Not one of the three knew how to swim, but they were going across the river, nevertheless. A thin thread of smoke beyond the bend on the other side of the river told them that the Indians were at work on a birch-bark canoe.

© GREAT SOURCE. ALL RIGHTS RESERVED.

Step 2: Organize important details.

Create a graphic organizer that can help you keep track of the setting clues you find.

Directions: Complete this Setting Chart for *Caddie Woodlawn*.

Setting Chart

Clues about time	Clues about place
Year:	Where the story takes place:
Season:	
Day of the week:	Specific details about the place:
Time of day:	

Step 3: Draw conclusions about the mood.

The setting can affect the mood, or atmosphere, of a story. For example, a story that takes place at midnight in a dark and forbidding castle will probably have a gloomy or fearful mood.

© GREAT SOURCE. ALL RIGHTS RESERVED.

Directions: In the left-hand column, write sentences from *Caddie Woodlawn* that describe the setting. In the right-hand column, write your thoughts about the mood of the writing.

Double-entry Journal

Sentences from the story	My thoughts about the mood

(Write two sentences from the story here.)   (Describe the mood here.)

Step 4: Draw conclusions about the characters.

Watch how the main character interacts with the setting. This can help you understand his or her personality.

Inference Chart

What Caddie says or does that relates to the setting	What this tells me about her

© GREAT SOURCE. ALL RIGHTS RESERVED.

Fiction

Focus on Dialogue

When reading dialogue, listen to what the speaker says.
Pay attention to how he or she says it.

Step 1: Do a careful reading.

Begin by reading slowly and carefully.

Directions: Read this excerpt from *Cheaper by the Dozen*. In this
scene, Dad plays a trick on his children, who are all recovering
from the measles.

who is talking:
....
....
....

from *Cheaper by the Dozen* by Frank Gilbreth, Jr.

Dad spent considerable time with us, joining in the
songs and all the games except pillow fights, which were
illegal. He still believed in letting sick children alone,
but with all of us sick—or all but Martha, at any
rate—he became so lonesome he couldn't stay away.

He came into the wards one night after supper,
and took a chair over in a corner. We noticed that his
face was covered with spots.

"Daddy," asked Anne, "what's the matter with
you? You're all broken out in spots."

"You're imagining things," said Dad, smirking.
"I'm all right."

"You've got the measles."

"I'm all right," said Dad. "I can take it."

"Daddy's got the measles, Daddy's got the
measles." Dad sat there grinning, but our shouts were enough to
bring Grandma on the run.

"What's the matter here?" she asked. And then to Dad, "Mercy sakes,
Frank, you're covered with spots."

"It's just a joke," Dad told his mother, weakly.

"Get yourself to bed. A man your age ought to know better. Shame
on you."

what they are saying:
....
....
....
....
....
....

© GREAT SOURCE. ALL RIGHTS RESERVED.

from *Cheaper by the Dozen*, continued

Grandma fumbled down her dress and put on her glasses. She peered into Dad's face.

"I declare, Frank Gilbreth," she told him, "sometimes I think you're more trouble than all of your children. Red ink! And you think it's a joke to scare a body half to death. Red ink!"

How they are saying it:

Step 2: Record your thoughts.

Next, record your thoughts about the dialogue. What are the characters saying? How are they saying it?

Directions: Reread these lines and record your thoughts.

Double-entry Journal

Dialogue	My thoughts
"You're imagining things," said Dad, smirking. "I'm all right."	
"I declare, Frank Gilbreth," she told him, "sometimes I think you're more trouble than all of your children. Red ink! . . ."	

Step 3: Search for clues about character.

Use the dialogue to help you make inferences about the characters.

© GREAT SOURCE. ALL RIGHTS RESERVED.

Directions: Write your inferences about Dad and Grandma here. Explain your evidence or "proof" from the dialogue.

◀ **Inference Chart**

Character	Personality	Proof
Dad		
Grandma		

Step 4: Search for clues about plot.

In their conversations with each other, characters often give clues about what has happened in the past and what may happen in the future. Keep an eye out for these important clues about plot. They can sharpen your understanding of a story.

© GREAT SOURCE. ALL RIGHTS RESERVED.

Directions: Predict what you think will happen next in *Cheaper by the Dozen*. Then explain your prediction.

My prediction:

Explanation:

Step 5: Look for clues about mood.

Dialogue can affect a story's mood.

Directions: Review the definition for mood on page 258 of your handbook. Then sketch the scene from *Cheaper by the Dozen*. Finish by writing a short description of the mood of this scene.

Sketch

The mood is

© GREAT SOURCE. ALL RIGHTS RESERVED.

Fiction

Focus on Plot

Plot is the actions or series of events the author describes. Follow these steps to understand a plot.

Step 1: Find the conflict.

The conflict is the main problem the characters must solve.

Directions: Read this fairy tale. Make notes about the conflict on the sticky note.

"The Little Match Girl" retold from Hans Christian Andersen

Long ago, on the last evening of the year, a poor little girl, bareheaded, and with naked feet, wandered the city. She carried a quantity of matches in an old apron, and she held a bundle of them in her hand. Nobody had bought anything from her the whole livelong day. No one had given her a single coin.

The little girl crept along trembling with cold and hunger. From all the windows the candles were gleaming, and every street smelled so deliciously of roast goose. The poor little match girl peeked in the windows and sighed with envy. She saw everything, but no one saw her. No one paid her a bit of attention.

In a corner formed by two houses, she seated herself down. She drew her feet close up to her, but she grew colder and colder. She dared not go home, for she had sold no matches and could not bring any money to her father.

Her little hands were almost numbed with cold. She wished with all her heart that she might take one match from her bundle, draw it against the wall, and warm her fingers by it.

She sat thinking about the match until she could stand it no longer. So she drew one out of the bunch and "Rsssst!", how it blazed, how it burned! It was a warm, bright flame, like a candle, and she held her hands over it. It seemed really to the little maiden as though she were sitting before a large iron stove—that's how warm and wonderful it was. But after another

what is the conflict?

© GREAT SOURCE. ALL RIGHTS RESERVED.

◁ **"The Little Match Girl,"** continued ▷

moment, the small flame went out, the stove vanished, and she had only the remains of the burnt-out match in her hand.

So she rubbed another match against the wall. It burned brightly, and where the light fell on the wall, she saw a brightly lit room, with a huge table in the center. On the table was spread a snow white tablecloth, and upon the tablecloth was a splendid roast goose that was steaming famously with its stuffing of apple and dried plums. But then the match went out and nothing but the thick, cold, damp wall was left behind.

So she lighted another match. Now she saw the most magnificent Christmas tree! Thousands of lights were burning on the green branches, and gaily colored pictures, such as she had seen in the shop-windows, looked down upon her. The little maiden stretched out her hands toward them when—but the match went out.

She drew another match against the wall. It was light once again, and there in the light stood her beloved old grandmother, who had died some years before.

"Grandmother!" cried the little one. "Oh, take me with you! Please don't go away when the match burns out! I'm afraid you'll vanish like the warm stove, the delicious roast goose, and the magnificent Christmas tree!" And so she rubbed the whole bundle of matches quickly against the wall, for she wanted to be quite sure of keeping her grandmother near her. And the matches gave such a brilliant light that it was brighter than at noon-day. The little match girl gazed upon her grandmother's face and the grandmother took the little maiden on her arm, and both flew in brightness and in joy so high, so very high, up to where there was no hunger or cold, only warm light and happiness.

But in the corner, at the cold hour of dawn, sat the poor girl, with rosy cheeks and a smiling mouth, leaning against the wall—frozen to death on the last evening of the old year. Stiff and stark sat the child there with her matches, of which one bundle had been burnt. "She wanted to warm herself," people said. No one had the slightest idea of what beautiful things she had seen; no one even dreamed of the splendor in which she, with her grandmother, had entered on the joys of a new year.

Step 2: Track key events.

Next, figure out the most important events in the plot.

© GREAT SOURCE. ALL RIGHTS RESERVED.

Fiction

Directions: Use a Story Organizer to record your thoughts.

◄ **Story Organizer**

Beginning	Middle	End

Step 3: Think about the theme.

The events of a plot can give you clues about the writer's theme.

Directions: Complete this Theme Diagram for "The Little Match Girl."

◄ **Theme Diagram**

Topic: a hungry, freezing girl

Detail #1:

Detail #2:

Detail #3:

Theme:

© GREAT SOURCE. ALL RIGHTS RESERVED.

Focus on Theme

Theme is a writer's message or statement about life. Here is a three-step plan that can help you make inferences about the theme of a work.

Step 1: Find the "big ideas" in the work.

First, think about the "big ideas," or important topics, in the work.

Directions: Read this excerpt from the novel *Black Beauty*. Make notes on the sticky notes.

from Black Beauty by Anna Sewell

There were six young colts in the meadow besides me; they were older than I was; some were nearly as large as grown-up horses. I used to run with them, and had great fun; we used to gallop all together round and round the field as hard as we could go. Sometimes we had rather rough play, for they would frequently bite and kick as well as gallop.

One day, when there was a good deal of kicking, my mother whinnied to me to come to her, and then she said:

"I wish you to pay attention to what I am going to say to you. The colts who live here are very good colts, but they are cart-horse colts, and of course they have not learned manners. You have been well-bred and well-born; your father has a great name in these parts, and your grandfather won the cup two years at the Newmarket races; your grandmother had the sweetest temper of any horse I ever knew, and I think you have never seen me kick or bite. I hope you will grow up gentle and good, and never learn bad ways; do your work with a good will, lift your feet up well when you trot, and never bite or kick even in play."

I have never forgotten my mother's advice; I knew she was a wise old horse, and our master thought a great deal of her. Her name was Duchess, but he often called her Pet.

Our master was a good, kind man. He gave us good food, good lodging, and kind words; he spoke as kindly to us as he did to his little children. We were all fond of him, and my mother loved him very much. When she saw

© GREAT SOURCE. ALL RIGHTS RESERVED.

NAME

FOR USE WITH PAGES 267–274

from Black Beauty, continued

him at the gate she would neigh with joy, and trot up to him. He would pat and stroke her and say, "Well, old Pet, and how is your little Darkie?" I was a dull black, so he called me Darkie; then he would give me a piece of bread, which was very good, and sometimes he brought a carrot for my mother. All the horses would come to him, but I think we were his favorites. My mother always took him to the town on a market day in a light gig.

There was a plowboy, Dick, who sometimes came into our field to pluck blackberries from the hedge. When he had eaten all he wanted he would have what he called fun with the colts, throwing stones and sticks at them to make them gallop. We did not much mind him, for we could gallop off; but sometimes a stone would hit and hurt us.

One day he was at this game, and did not know that the master was in the next field; but he was there, watching what was going on; over the hedge he jumped in a snap, and catching Dick by the arm, he gave him such a box on the ear as made him roar with the pain and surprise. As soon as we saw the master we trotted up nearer to see what went on.

"Bad boy!" he said, "bad boy! to chase the colts. This is not the first time, nor the second, but it shall be the last. There—take your money and go home; I shall not want you on my farm again." So we never saw Dick any more. Old Daniel, the man who looked after the horses, was just as gentle as our master, so we were well off.

This story seems to be about:

Here are some of the big ideas:

Step 2: Note what the characters do or say.

Next, make a connection between the characters and the big ideas.

© GREAT SOURCE. ALL RIGHTS RESERVED.

Directions: Read these lines from *Black Beauty*. Tell how they relate to the big ideas you listed on the sticky note.

Double-entry Journal

Quote	What I Think about It
"You have been well-bred and well-born; your father has a great name in these parts. . . ."	
"Bad boy!" he said, "bad boy! to chase the colts. This is not the first time, nor the second, but it shall be the last."	

Step 3: Decide on the author's message.

The theme is the point the author wants to make about the topic.

Directions: Use information from Steps 1 and 2 for this organizer.

Theme Diagram

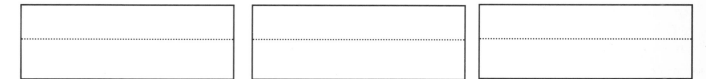

1. Big idea kindness

2. What the characters do and say

3. What the author wants to teach me

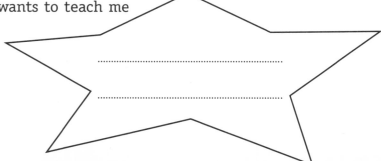

© GREAT SOURCE. ALL RIGHTS RESERVED.

Fiction

Focus on Authors

Read two or more works by a single author. Then choose an element to compare, such as the characters, plot, setting, or theme. Here you'll compare characters.

Step 1: Read.

Use the reading process to help you read and understand the author's characters.

Directions: Read these three excerpts from novels by Roald Dahl. Make notes on the stickies.

from *The Magic Finger* by Roald Dahl

For months I had been telling myself that I would never put the Magic Finger upon anyone again—not after what happened to my teacher, old Mrs. Winter.

Poor old Mrs. Winter.

One day we were in class, and she was teaching us spelling. "Stand up," she said to me, "and spell cat."

"That's an easy one," I said. *"K-a-t."*

"You are a stupid little girl!" Mrs. Winter said.

"I am not a stupid little girl!" I cried. "I am a very nice little girl!"

"Go and stand in the corner," Mrs. Winter said.

Then I got cross, and I saw red, and I put the Magic Finger on Mrs. Winter good and strong, and almost at once. . . .

Guess what?

Whiskers began growing out of her face!

This is what I know about the narrator:

....

....

....

....

© GREAT SOURCE. ALL RIGHTS RESERVED.

from *Fantastic Mr. Fox* by Roald Dahl

There was no food for the foxes that night, and soon the children dozed off. Then Mrs. Fox dozed off. But Mr. Fox couldn't sleep because of the pain in the stump of his tail. "Well," he thought, "I suppose I'm lucky to be alive at all. And now they've found our hole, we're going to have to move out as soon as possible. We'll never get any peace if we . . . What was *that*?" He turned his head sharply and listened. The noise he heard now was the most frightening noise a fox can ever hear—the scrape-scrape-scraping of shovels digging into the soil.

"Wake up!" he shouted. "They're digging us out!"

Mrs. Fox was wide awake in one second. She sat up, quivering all over. "Are you sure that's it?" she whispered.

"I'm positive! Listen!"

"They'll kill my children!" cried Mrs. Fox.

"Never!" said Mr. Fox.

This is what I know about Mr. Fox:

_____

_____

_____

_____

_____

from *Charlie and the Chocolate Factory* by Roald Dahl

Very slowly, Charlie's fingers began to tear open one small corner of the wrapping paper.

The old people in the bed all leaned forward, craning their scraggy necks.

Then suddenly, as though he couldn't bear the suspense any longer, Charlie tore the wrapper right down the middle . . . and on to his lap, there fell . . . a light-brown creamy-colored chocolate candy bar.

There was no sign of a Golden Ticket anywhere.

"Well—that's *that*!" said Grandpa Joe brightly. "It's just what we expected."

Charlie looked up. Four kind old faces were watching him intently from the bed. He smiled at them, a small sad smile, and then he shrugged his shoulders and picked up the candy bar and held it out to his mother, and said, "Here, Mother, have a bit. We'll share it. I want everybody to taste it."

© GREAT SOURCE. ALL RIGHTS RESERVED.

Fiction

from *Charlie and the Chocolate Factory*, continued

"Certainly not!" his mother said.

And the others all cried, "No, no! We wouldn't dream of it! It's *all* yours!"

"*Please,*" begged Charlie, turning around and offering it to Grandpa Joe.

But neither he nor anyone else would take even a tiny bite.

This is what I know about

Charlie:

....

....

Step 2: Make inferences.

Next, make inferences (reasonable guesses) about the characters.

Directions: Write your inferences about the three characters on this chart.

Inference Chart

Character	What I Know	What I've Inferred
The narrator in *The Magic Finger*		
Mr. Fox		
Charlie		

© GREAT SOURCE. ALL RIGHTS RESERVED.

NAME ....

Step 3: Compare and contrast.

Then compare and contrast the three characters.

Directions: Complete this Venn Diagram. Use information from the chart.

Venn Diagram

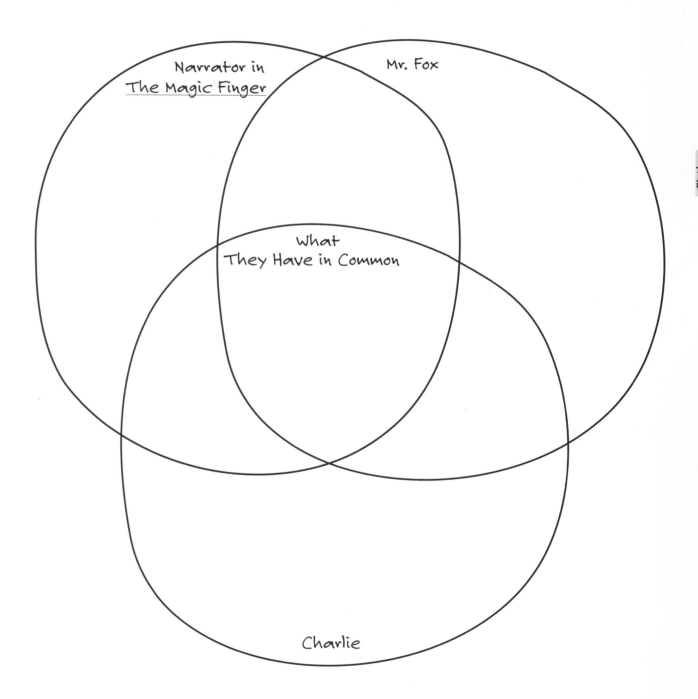

Narrator in
<u>The Magic Finger</u>

Mr. Fox

What
They Have in Common

Charlie

© GREAT SOURCE. ALL RIGHTS RESERVED.

Fiction

Step 4: Draw conclusions.

After you finish your comparison, draw some conclusions.

Directions: Complete this organizer. Refer to your Venn Diagram.

Main Idea Organizer

Main Idea		
Detail 1	Detail 2	Detail 3
Conclusion		

Write details that support the main idea here.

Step 5: Report.

Writing what you've learned can help you remember it.

Directions: Write a journal entry about the three characters. Explain how the characters are similar or different. If you like, include notes about other Roald Dahl characters you know.

Journal Entry

© GREAT SOURCE. ALL RIGHTS RESERVED.

Reading a Poem

Think of a poem as a song. The sound of the words is as important as their meaning. Your job when reading a poem is to "listen" to the music of the words and figure out what they mean.

Before Reading

Use the reading process and the strategy of close reading to help you understand a well-known poem by Rudyard Kipling.

A Set a Purpose

You have two main purposes when reading a poem:

• Find out what the poem is saying.

• Figure out what makes the poem memorable.

• **To set your purpose, ask questions about the meaning of the poem and the things that make it special.**

Directions: Write two purpose questions for reading Kipling's "If—." Then tell your own opinion of poetry. What do you like about it? What do you dislike?

Purpose question #1:

Purpose question #2:

This is what I like about poetry:

This is what I don't like:

© GREAT SOURCE. ALL RIGHTS RESERVED.

Poetry

B Preview

First, preview the poem you're about to read. Look for the name of the poet and the title of the poem. Check for rhyme and repeated words. Then read the first and last lines carefully. Try to get a general sense of what the poem is about.

Directions: Preview "If—." Make notes on this chart.

◀ Preview Notes

The title of the poem is:
....

The poet's name is:
....

This is what I noticed about the shape of the poem:
....

....

This is what came to mind when I read the first line:
....

....

This is what I noticed when I read the last line:
....

....

I saw these rhyming words:
....

....

I saw these repeated words and phrases:
....

....

© GREAT SOURCE. ALL RIGHTS RESERVED.

"If—" by Rudyard Kipling

If you can keep your head when all about you
    Are losing theirs and blaming it on you;
If you can trust yourself when all men doubt you,
    But make allowance for their doubting too;
If you can wait and not be tired by waiting,
    Or being lied about, don't deal in lies,
Or being hated, don't give way to hating,
    And yet don't look too good, nor talk too wise;

If you can dream—and not make dreams your master;
    If you can think—and not make thoughts your aim;
If you can meet with Triumph and Disaster
    And treat those two impostors just the same;
If you can bear to hear the truth you've spoken
    Twisted by knaves to make a trap for fools,
Or watch the things you gave your life to, broken,
    And stoop and build 'em up with worn-out tools;

If you can make one heap of all your winnings
    And risk it on one turn of pitch-and-toss,
And lose, and start again at your beginnings
    And never breathe a word about your loss;
If you can force your heart and nerve and sinew
    To serve your turn long after they are gone,
And so hold on when there is nothing in you
    Except the Will which says to them: "Hold on!"

If you can talk with crowds and keep your virtue,
    Or walk with Kings—nor lose the common touch,
If neither foes nor loving friends can hurt you,
    If all men count with you, but none too much;
If you can fill the unforgiving minute
    With sixty seconds' worth of distance run,
Yours is the Earth and everything that's in it,
    And—which is more—you'll be a Man, my son!

What repeated words do you see?

What inferences can you make about the speaker of the poem?

What do you think is the speaker's message?

Poetry

© GREAT SOURCE. ALL RIGHTS RESERVED.

 **Plan**

The strategy of close reading can help you hear the music and understand the meaning of individual lines in the poem. Plan on reading the poem at least three times.

• **When you do a close reading of a poem, you read for enjoyment, meaning, and important elements such as rhyme and rhythm.**

During Reading

D Read with a Purpose

On your first reading of a poem, read for enjoyment. On your second reading, read for meaning. Ask yourself, "What is the poet's message?" On your third reading, read for structure and tone.

Directions: Read Kipling's poem three times. Make notes on this chart.

Plan for Reading a Poem

First Reading	Second Reading	Third Reading
Here's what I liked about the poem:	I think Kipling's message is this:	Here's what I noticed about the rhyme:
		rhythm:
		tone:

© GREAT SOURCE. ALL RIGHTS RESERVED.

Using the Strategy

Close reading means reading word-for-word and line-for-line. Use a Double-entry Journal to keep track of your thoughts and feelings about individual lines and words. Use a Two Per Line to explore meaning.

• **Record your close reading ideas on a Double-entry Journal and a Two Per Line.**

Directions: Read these quotes from Kipling's poem. Then write how they make you feel.

Double-entry Journal

Quote	My Thoughts about It
"If you can trust yourself when all men doubt you, / But make allowance for their doubting too;"	
"If you can bear to hear the truth you've spoken"	
"If you can fill the unforgiving minute / With sixty seconds' worth of distance run,"	
"Yours is the Earth and everything that's in it, / And—which is more— you'll be a Man, my son!"	

© GREAT SOURCE. ALL RIGHTS RESERVED.

Poetry

Directions: Reread the second stanza in Kipling's poem. Write two important words from each line in the poem. Then write your thoughts about the meaning of those words.

◀ **Two Per Line**

Text	My Ideas

© GREAT SOURCE. ALL RIGHTS RESERVED.

Understanding How Poems Are Organized

Poets make all kinds of choices. Here are two of the most important:

- To write with or without rhyme

- To write with or without shapes and structures

Directions: Do a close reading of this stanza. Then answer the questions on the sticky notes and on the lines below.

from "If—" by Rudyard Kipling

If you can talk with crowds and keep your virtue,
   Or walk with Kings—not lose the common touch,
If neither foes nor loving friends can hurt you,
   If all men count with you, but none too much;
If you can fill the unforgiving minute
   With sixty seconds' worth of distance run,
Yours is the Earth and everything that's in it,
   And—which is more—you'll be a Man, my son!

This poem has ____ stanzas.

This is stanza ____ .

It has ____ lines.

Poetry

1. This is what I noticed about the poem's shape and structure:

_____

_____

2. Here are rhyming words in the stanza:

_____

_____

3. The most important lines in the stanza are:

_____

_____

_____

_____

© GREAT SOURCE. ALL RIGHTS RESERVED.

E Connect

When you read a poem, think about how the subject and message relate to your own thoughts and ideas.

• **Think about how the poem connects with your own experiences.**

<u>Directions:</u> Answer these "connection" questions.

◀ Connecting to a Poem

The speaker of the poem	The advice from "If—" that really
reminds me of	applies to me:
because	
	because

After Reading

Always spend a few minutes collecting your thoughts about the poem you've just read.

F Pause and Reflect

To reflect, think about the purpose questions you wrote before reading.

• **Ask yourself, "How well did I meet my purpose?"**

© GREAT SOURCE. ALL RIGHTS RESERVED.

Directions: Answer these two purpose questions on the lines below.

Purpose question #1: What is "If—" about? What is the poet's message?

Purpose question #2:

 **Reread**

If you're still not sure about the poem's meaning, do some rereading.

• **A powerful rereading strategy to use with poetry is paraphrasing.**

Directions: Read the lines in Column 1. Rewrite the lines in your own words in Column 2. Write your thoughts about the lines in Column 3.

◄ **Paraphrase or Retelling Chart**

Lines	My Paraphrase	My Thoughts
"Or being hated, don't give way to hating . . ."		
"And lose, and start again at your beginnings / And never breathe a word about your loss . . ."		

© GREAT SOURCE. ALL RIGHTS RESERVED.

 Remember

It's easy to remember a poem if it has meaning in your own life.

• **Writing your own version of a poem can help you remember it.**

Directions: On the lines below, write a four-line stanza that follows the same rhythmic pattern Kipling uses in "If—."

Journal Entry

© GREAT SOURCE. ALL RIGHTS RESERVED.

Focus on Language

Most poets have a masterful command of language. They know how to choose words that can help you see, hear, smell, touch, and even taste what is being described. Follow these steps when focusing on a poem's language.

Step 1: Read and take notes.

First read the poem all the way through without stopping. Then read it again. Mark the words that catch your attention.

Directions: Read this poem. Circle words that seem important or interesting to you.

"The Cow" by Robert Louis Stevenson

The friendly cow all red and white,
    I love with all my heart:
She gives me cream with all her might,
    To eat with apple tart.

She wanders lowing here and there,
    And yet she cannot stray,
All in the pleasant open air,
    The pleasant light of day;

And blown by all the winds that pass
    And wet with all the showers,
She walks among the meadow grass
    And eats the meadow flowers.

© GREAT SOURCE. ALL RIGHTS RESERVED.

Poetry

Step 2: Learn the words you don't know.

Next, circle words in the poem that you don't know. Define them using context clues or a dictionary.

Directions: Make a list of words in "The Cow" that you don't know. Try defining the words in context. If this doesn't work, use a dictionary.

List

Words	Definitions

Step 3: Look for figurative language.

Many of the poems you read will contain personification, which is one type of figurative language.

Directions: Review pages 312–313 in your handbook. Then find an example of personification in "The Cow." Write what you find on the chart.

Chart

Personification (human qualities given to something that isn't human)

Example from the poem:

© GREAT SOURCE. ALL RIGHTS RESERVED.

Step 4: Look for imagery.

An image is a mental picture. It is what you "see" in your mind as you read. You can spot imagery in a poem if you look for words that relate to the five senses: sight, hearing, smell, touch, and taste.

Directions: Find examples of sensory language in "The Cow." Record what you find on the chart.

Chart

Sight Words	Hearing Words	Smell Words	Touch Words	Taste Words
red				
white				

Step 5: Draw what you "see."

Visualizing what the poet describes makes the poem easier to understand.

Directions: Look at the sensory words you listed on the chart. Then draw a picture of what you "see."

Sketch

© GREAT SOURCE. ALL RIGHTS RESERVED.

Poetry

Focus on Meaning

Sometimes a poem's meaning is easy to understand. Other times, you'll have to search for clues. Follow these steps.

Step 1: Read for the subject.

First, read the poem slowly, but without stopping. Try to get an idea of what it is about.

Directions: Read these stanzas from a famous poem called "Solitude." Make notes on the stickies.

"Solitude" by Ella Wheeler Wilcox

Laugh, and the world laughs with you;
Weep, and you weep alone;
    For the sad old earth
    Must borrow its mirth,
It has trouble enough of its own.

Sing, and the hills will answer;
Sigh, it is lost on the air;
    The echoes bound
    To a joyful sound,
But shrink from voicing care.

Rejoice, and men will seek you;
Grieve, and they turn and go;
    They want full measure
    Of all your pleasure,
But they do not need your woe.

Be glad, and your friends are many;
Be sad, and you lose them all;
    There are none to decline
    Your nectared wine,
But alone you must drink life's gall.

This poem is about
....

....

....

I noticed these repeated
words in the first stanza:

....

I noticed these repeated
words in the second
stanza:

© GREAT SOURCE. ALL RIGHTS RESERVED.

Step 2: Consider what's unusual and important.

Next, look for unusual and important words or ideas.

Directions: Circle one or two key words in each line of the first stanza. Write the words you circled on this chart. Then describe the "picture" these words paint and what they make you think about.

◁ Two Per Line

Key Word	My Ideas
Line 1 laugh /world	
Line 2	
Line 3	
Line 4	
Line 5	
Line 6	
Line 7	
Line 8	

(Write your key words here.)   (Describe what the words make you think about here.)

(If you like, make a Two Per Line Organizer for the second stanza on a separate piece of paper.)

© GREAT SOURCE. ALL RIGHTS RESERVED.

Poetry

145

Step 3: Connect.

Pay attention to how the words of a poem make you feel. This can help you figure out the poem's meaning.

Directions: Answer this question about "Solitude."

How did you feel as you were reading the poem?

....

....

....

....

Step 4: Tell the poem's meaning.

The meaning of a poem is often a statement about life.

Directions: Write the subject of "Solitude." Then tell what you think the poem means.

Subject of the poem:

....

....

....

The statement about life that the poet is making:

....

....

....

© GREAT SOURCE. ALL RIGHTS RESERVED.

Focus on Sound and Shape

Studying the sound and shape of a poem can help you understand the poet's meaning. Follow these steps.

Step 1: Listen for rhyme.

On your first reading, listen for words that rhyme.

Directions: Read this part of "Calico Pie" by Edward Lear. Make notes on the stickies.

from "Calico Pie" by Edward Lear

I.

     Calico Pie,
     The little Birds fly,
Down to the calico tree,
     Their wings were blue,
     And they sang "Tilly-loo!"
     Till away they flew,—
And they never came back to me!
They never came back!
They never came back!
     They never came back to me!

II.

     Calico Jam,
     The little Fish swam,
Over the syllabub sea,
     He took off his hat,
     To the Sole and the Sprat,
     And the Willeby-wat,—
But he never came back to me!
He never came back!
He never came back!
     He never came back to me!

This poem has
stanzas.

These words rhyme
in stanza 1:

These lines rhyme in
stanza 2:

© GREAT SOURCE. ALL RIGHTS RESERVED.

Poetry

Step 2: Hear the rhythm.

Next, listen for the rhythm or "beat" of the poem.

Directions: Reread page 325 of your handbook. Then read the stressed and unstressed syllables in these three lines from "Calico Pie." Tell what the poem sounds like to you.

Listening for Rhythm

Cálico Pie,

The líttle Birds fly,

Dówn to the cálico tree,

This poem sounds like ....

Step 3: Look for the shape and organization.

Always look at the shape of a poem on the page. How are the words and lines arranged? Is there repetition? These questions can give you clues about meaning.

Directions: Reread "Calico Pie." Then answer the questions.

Questions

1. What is the poem's shape? ....

....

2. What is the subject of the first stanza? ....

3. What is the subject of the second? ....

4. What repeated lines can you find? ....

....

....

....

....

© GREAT SOURCE. ALL RIGHTS RESERVED.

Reading a Play

Think of a play as a long conversation between two or more characters. As you read, "listen" to what the characters are saying. Make inferences about how they are feeling.

Before Reading

Use the reading process and the strategy of summarizing to help you read and respond to an excerpt from *Rip Van Winkle: A Play.*

A Set a Purpose

In order to understand a play, you must understand the characters, plot, and theme.

- **To set your purpose, ask questions about important literary elements in the play.**

Directions: Write your purpose for reading *Rip Van Winkle: A Play* here. Then tell what you already know about this story.

Purpose question #1: ....

....

Purpose question #2: ....

....

Purpose question #3: ....

....

What I know about the story: ....

....

....

© GREAT SOURCE. ALL RIGHTS RESERVED.

Drama

B Preview

When you preview a play, look at the title, the name of the playwright, the cast of characters, and the information about setting. Begin with the title page.

- **Previewing a play helps you know what to expect when it comes time to do your careful reading.**

Directions: Preview this title page for *Rip Van Winkle: A Play*. Make notes on the stickies.

Rip Van Winkle
A Play

Based on the short story "Rip Van Winkle" by Washington Irving

Cast of Characters
In order of appearance

RIP VAN WINKLE
the INNKEEPER
an OLD MAN
JULIA GARDENIER
an OLD WOMAN

The title of the play is ....

....

There are ....

characters.

Setting
Time: the late 1700s, shortly after the Revolutionary War
Place: a small New England town at the base of the Catskill Mountains

This comes to mind when I read the
information about the setting:

Here's what I noticed after
skimming the first several lines:

© GREAT SOURCE. ALL RIGHTS RESERVED.

Rip Van Winkle: A Play

Act II

(SCENE: A New England town at the base of the Catskill Mountains. The Revolutionary War has just ended, so there is red, white, and blue bunting hanging from the houses and the storefronts. RIP VAN WINKLE stands on the street in front of a large inn. There is a merry crowd gathered on the porch. RIP stands watching for a moment or two. He has a decidedly puzzled air about him.)

RIP [TO HIMSELF]: Hmmm. Things are becoming stranger and stranger. First, I find that my brand-new gun is rusted solid, as if it's been out of doors for twenty years. Now I find myself at the King George Inn—my home away from home—and I know not a soul! In fact, I barely recognize the inn itself. *(Looking up and then down.)* There's a new roof and a new porch and there are red, white, and blue banners hanging from every window. And there—where the picture of good King George used to hang—is a portrait of a "General Washington"! What could it mean?

(Eventually, the crowd on the porch catches sight of RIP and the odd figure he cuts. Men and women stop their conversations mid-sentence and stare boldly at the funny old man with the gray beard who is standing in front of them. Noticing their attention, RIP clears his throat and addresses the crowd.)

RIP [IN A VOICE THAT SOUNDS LIKE IT HASN'T BEEN USED IN YEARS]: Good people! A moment of your time, if you will. I've had a rather unfortunate night, and I wonder if someone might come to my aid.

INNKEEPER [A BIT IMPATIENTLY]: Well, what is it, old man? I'm the keeper of this fair place, and I suppose I might be of some assistance to you. But mind you, you'll have to state your business quickly. I'm in no frame of mind to stand here jawin' all day with an old geezer like yourself.

RIP [MIGHTILY OFFENDED]: Geezer? Well, what on earth do you mean, my good man? I'm as young, hale, and hearty as you!

(The crowd laughs at RIP's response. Some of the men pull at their beards and stick their tongues in their cheeks. When he sees what the men are doing, RIP pulls at his own beard and sticks his own tongue in his cheek. It is then that he discovers that his beard—which he had combed through the day before—had gone gray and was easily a foot long.)

RIP [ASTONISHED]: But what's this? My beard—I don't—

© GREAT SOURCE. ALL RIGHTS RESERVED.

Rip Van Winkle: A Play, continued

Stop and Record

Fill in the "Beginning" section of your Story Organizer (page 155).

INNKEEPER [IRRITABLY]: I told you to be quick about it, old man. What do you need from me?

RIP [MAKING AN EFFORT TO IGNORE HIS BEARD]: Well, sir, I was wondering if you could tell me where my friends are.

INNKEEPER: Well—Who are they?—Name them.

RIP [THOUGHTFULLY]: Well. Where's Nicholas Vedder?

(The crowd is silent for a moment or two. Then an OLD MAN replies, in a thin, piping voice.)

OLD MAN: Nicholas Vedder! Why he is dead and gone these eighteen years! There was a wooden tombstone in the church-yard that used to tell all about him, but that's rotten and gone too.

RIP: And Brom Dutcher? Where is he?

OLD MAN: Oh, he went off to the army in the beginning of the war; some say he was killed at the storming of Stony Point—others say he was drowned in a squall at the foot of Antony's Nose. I don't know—he never came back again.

RIP [MORE URGENTLY]: Where's Van Bummel, the schoolmaster?

OLD MAN: He went off to the wars too, was a great militia general, and is now in Congress.

(RIP sinks to the ground at this final piece of news. His heart is broken by the sad changes the OLD MAN has described. Still, he manages to find the courage to address the crowd once more.)

RIP [IN DESPAIR]: Does nobody here know Rip Van Winkle?

INNKEEPER [GLAD TO BE OF SERVICE AT LAST]: Oh, Rip Van Winkle! Oh, to be sure! That's Rip Van Winkle yonder, leaning against the tree.

(RIP rises to his feet and looks in the direction of the man's pointed finger.)

© GREAT SOURCE. ALL RIGHTS RESERVED.

Rip Van Winkle: A Play, continued

RIP [IN CONFUSION]: Yes, there is a man—exactly as I looked before my nap. It is the lazy, messy Rip Van Winkle that is known to the whole town. But—but—how can this be? God knows, I'm not myself—I'm somebody else—that's me yonder—no—that's somebody else got into my shoes—I was myself last night, but I fell asleep on the mountain, and they've changed my gun, and everything's changed, and I'm changed, and I can't tell what's my name, or who I am!

Stop and Record

Make some notes in the "Middle" section of your Story Organizer (page 155).

(The crowd now begins to look at each other, nod, wink significantly, and tap their fingers against their foreheads. There is a whisper also, about securing the gun, and keeping the old fellow from doing mischief. At this critical moment, a fresh, comely woman presses through the crowd to get a peep at what was happening. She has a chubby child in her arms who is squirming in his fear of the gray-bearded man.)

WOMAN [TO THE CHILD]: "Hush, Rip. Hush, you little fool. The old man won't hurt you."

(The name of the child, the air of the mother, the tone of her voice all awaken in RIP a trail of recollections.)

RIP [EXCITEDLY]: What is your name, my good woman?
WOMAN [PLEASANTLY]: Judith Gardenier.
RIP: And your father's name?
WOMAN: Ah, poor man, Rip Van Winkle was his name, but it's twenty years since he went away from home with his gun, and never has been heard of since—his dog came home without him; but whether he shot himself, or was carried away by the Indians, nobody can tell. I was then but a little girl.

Stop and Record

Make some more notes in the "Middle" section of your Story Organizer (page 155).

© GREAT SOURCE. ALL RIGHTS RESERVED.

Drama

Rip Van Winkle: A Play, continued

RIP [SLOWLY NOW, IN A FALTERING VOICE]: Where's your mother?

WOMAN: Oh, she too had died but a short time since; she broke a blood-vessel in a fit of passion at a New England peddler.

(RIP breathes a sigh of relief when he realizes there will be no more scoldings from his wife. He opens his arms and draws close his daughter and the child in her arms.)

RIP [JOYFULLY]: But my good woman! I am your father! Young Rip Van Winkle once—old Rip Van Winkle now!—Does nobody know poor Rip Van Winkle?

(The crowd murmurs excitedly. Eventually, an OLD WOMAN totters out from among the crowd, puts her hand to her brow, and peers into Rip's eyes.)

OLD WOMAN [EXCITEDLY]: "Sure enough! It is Rip Van Winkle—it is himself! Welcome home again, old neighbor—Why, where have you been these twenty long years?

End of Act II

Stop and Record
Fill in the "End" section of your Story Organizer (page 155).

C Plan

After your preview, make a plan. Choose a reading strategy that can help you understand how the literary elements of characters, plot, and theme work in this play.

• **The strategy of summarizing can help you meet your purpose for reading a play.**

© GREAT SOURCE. ALL RIGHTS RESERVED.

During Reading

D Read with a Purpose

Now do a careful reading of *Rip Van Winkle: A Play*. Write your notes on a Story Organizer.

Directions: Make notes on this Story Organizer as you read.

Story Organizer

Beginning	Middle	End

© GREAT SOURCE. ALL RIGHTS RESERVED.

Drama

Using the Strategy

When you summarize a play, you use your own words to retell the main events of the plot. You also tell your ideas about character and theme.

• **Summarizing can help you understand and remember what you've read.**

Directions: Complete this Web. Think of words that are attracted to the magnet term "Rip Van Winkle." Then use these words in a plot summary of the play.

Web

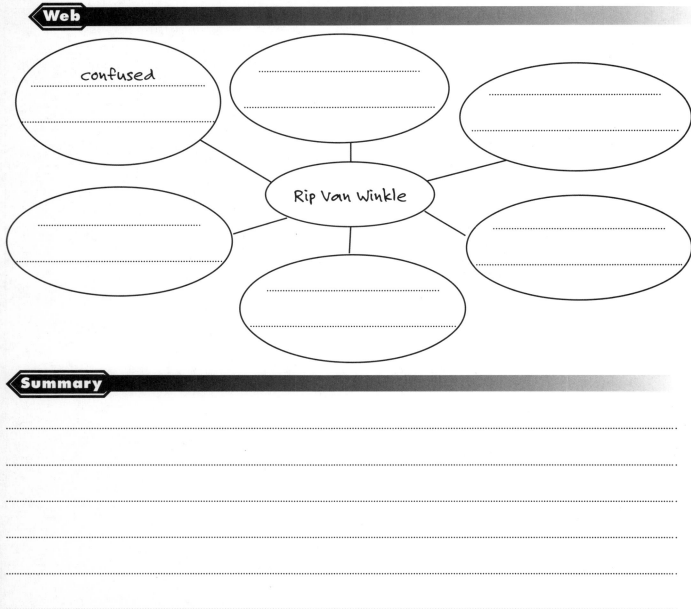

confused

Rip Van Winkle

Summary

....

....

....

....

....

....

....

© GREAT SOURCE. ALL RIGHTS RESERVED.

Understanding How Plays Are Organized

Most plays are organized around a central conflict. This is the problem the characters must resolve before the end.

• **To understand a play, think about its central conflict.**

Directions: Answer these questions about *Rip Van Winkle: A Play*. They can help you think about the central conflict of the play.

1. What is the main problem that Rip Van Winkle must solve?

....

....

2. How does Rip feel about the problem?

....

....

....

3. How is the problem resolved?

....

....

 **Connect**

Remember that active readers make connections between their own lives and what they're reading.

• **Making a connection to a play can help you understand its themes.**

Directions: Reread this passage from the play. Make notes on the sticky.

from *Rip Van Winkle: A Play*

RIP [IN CONFUSION]: Yes, there is a man—exactly as I looked before my nap. It is the lazy, messy Rip Van Winkle that is known to the whole town. But—but—how can this be? God knows, I'm not myself—I'm somebody else—that's me yonder—no—that's somebody else got into my shoes—I was myself last night, but I fell asleep on the mountain, and they've changed my gun, and everything's changed, and I'm changed, and I can't tell what's my name, or who I am!

How do you feel about Rip Van Winkle?

....

....

....

© GREAT SOURCE. ALL RIGHTS RESERVED.

Directions: Next, explain your personal connection to the play.

Rip Van Winkle reminds me of ....

because ....

....

After Reading

When you finish reading, think about your original purpose.

F Pause and Reflect

Reread the purpose notes you made on page 149. Check to see if you've accomplished what you set out to do.

• **Ask yourself, "Have I met my purpose for reading?"**

Directions: Answer these questions about *Rip Van Winkle: A Play*.

Purpose Questions

What is the play about?	Who are the main characters and what are they like?
Can you describe what happens during the play?	Can you name the big ideas in this play?
What are some of the big ideas in the play?	
What do these big ideas mean?	

© GREAT SOURCE. ALL RIGHTS RESERVED.

G Reread

If you're having trouble with the theme of a play, you may need to do a little rereading. The strategy of questioning the author can help.

• **Questioning the author can help you find the theme.**

Directions: Read the three questions for the author on this Theme Diagram. Then write what you think the author would say in response.

◀ **Theme Diagram**

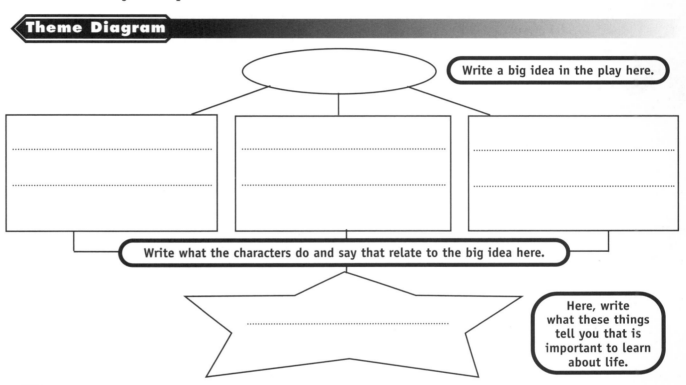

Write a big idea in the play here.

Write what the characters do and say that relate to the big idea here.

Here, write what these things tell you that is important to learn about life.

H Remember

Good readers remember what they've read.

• **To remember a play, respond to a key line or speech.**

Directions: Write a key line from *Rip Van Winkle: A Play*. Then tell what's important or interesting about this line.

Key line: ....

....

Why I chose it: ....

....

© GREAT SOURCE. ALL RIGHTS RESERVED.

Drama

Focus on Language

The reason a play's language might seem strange to you is that plays are meant to be spoken rather than read. When you do read a play, pay careful attention to the stage directions and dialogue. These can help you "see" and "hear" the action of the play.

Step 1: Read the stage directions.

Stage directions, which are the instructions to the actors and actresses, can give you important information about the play's setting.

Directions: Read these stage directions. Then sketch the scene.

> **from *Rip Van Winkle: A Play***
>
> (SCENE: A New England town at the base of the Catskill Mountains. The Revolutionary War has just ended, so there is red, white, and blue bunting hanging from the houses and the storefronts. RIP VAN WINKLE stands on the street in front of a large inn. There is a merry crowd gathered on the porch. RIP stands watching for a moment or two. He has a decidedly puzzled air about him.)

Sketch

© GREAT SOURCE. ALL RIGHTS RESERVED.

Step 2: Understand the dialogue.

The dialogue in a play can give you important clues about its characters—who they are, what they're like, how they feel about themselves, and how they feel about each other.

Directions: Read this conversation between Rip Van Winkle and his wife. Then make inferences about the two characters.

from *Rip Van Winkle: A Play*

DAME VAN WINKLE [SHAKING HER FINGER]: Husband, you are the laziest man I've ever known. You can sit all day upon a wet rock, a heavy fishing pole in your hand, and never make a single complaint. You can hunt for hours with a musket on your shoulder, trudging through woods and swamps, and up hill and down dale to shoot a few squirrels or wild pigeons. Yet when I ask you to lift a single finger to keep the farm in order, or to find a job to help support this family, you shake your head and shrug your shoulders and act helpless.

RIP [MEEKLY]: It is so, my dear. It is so. Ah, me.

Drama

My inferences about Dame Van Winkle: She is   and

My inferences about Rip: He is   and

© GREAT SOURCE. ALL RIGHTS RESERVED.

Step 3: Study key lines and speeches.

Every play has at least a few key lines and speeches. Examine these, and you'll find clues about the big ideas and theme.

Directions: Underline details in this speech that support the playwright's big idea of "change." Then write what you think the playwright is trying to tell you about change. What lesson about life is the writer trying to teach?

Inference Chart

Text	What the playwright is saying about "change"
from *Rip Van Winkle: A Play* RIP [TO HIMSELF]: Hmmm. Things are becoming stranger and stranger. First, I find that my brand-new gun is rusted solid, as if it's been out of doors for twenty years. Now I find myself at the King George Inn—my home away from home—and I know not a soul! In fact, I barely recognize the inn itself. *(Looking up and then down.)* There's a new roof and a new porch and there are red, white, and blue banners hanging from every window. And there—where the picture of good King George used to hang—is a portrait of a "General Washington"! What could it mean?	

© GREAT SOURCE. ALL RIGHTS RESERVED.

Focus on ⬭Theme⬭

A play's theme is the point the author wants to make. It is the main idea of the work. Use this plan to help you analyze a theme.

Step 1: Find the subject or "big ideas."

First, find the subject or big ideas in the play. Ask yourself, "*Who* or *what* is the playwright mostly talking about?"

Directions: Write two big ideas in *Rip Van Winkle: A Play.*

Big Ideas in *Rip Van Winkle*

Big idea #1	Big idea #2

Step 2: Note what the characters say and do.

Next, figure out the relationship between the characters and the big ideas. Pay attention to what they say and do.

Directions: Tell what the characters in *Rip Van Winkle: A Play* do and say that relates to the big ideas.

Big idea #1	Big idea #2
What the characters say or do:	What the characters say or do:

© GREAT SOURCE. ALL RIGHTS RESERVED.

Drama

Step 3: Figure out the playwright's message.

Don't confuse a play's subject with its theme. The **subject** is what the play is about. The **theme** is the playwright's *message* about the subject.

Example

Write the
subject here.

Surprises

What the playwright
says about it

Life is full of them.

My theme statement

A theme in Rip Van Winkle is that life is full of surprises.

+ ... **=**

Directions: Use this formula to find another theme in *Rip Van Winkle: A Play*. Then write whether or not you agree with the theme. Does it seem like a true statement about life?

Write the subject here.　　　　Write what the playwright
　　　　　　　　　　　　　　says about it.

.... **+** ....

Write a theme statement here.

= ....

....

Do you agree with this theme? Does it seem like a true statement about life?
....

....

....

....

....

© GREAT SOURCE. ALL RIGHTS RESERVED.

Reading a Website

The Internet can be one of the most fascinating—or frustrating—places you'll ever visit. Before visiting a website, figure out what you need to find and how you're going to find it. The reading process can help.

Before Reading

Practice using the reading process and the strategy of reading critically to help you navigate a kid's website about the World Series.

 ### A Set a Purpose

Ask yourself two questions: "Why am I at this site?" and "What do I want to find out?"

> **• To set your purpose, ask and answer questions about the website.**

Directions: Write two questions about the World Series website. Then answer them.

Purpose question #1: ....

My answer: ....

Purpose question #2: ....

My answer: ....

 ### B Preview

When you reach the site you want to use, do a quick preview. Try to refrain from clicking during your preview. Concentrate on checking to see if this site has information that can help you meet your purpose.

> **• Previewing a website beforehand lets you see what the site has to offer.**

© GREAT SOURCE. ALL RIGHTS RESERVED.

Internet

Directions: Preview the World Series for Kids website. Pay attention to the items on this checklist. Make notes on what you find.

Drawing Conclusions

Preview Items	My Notes
✔ The site name and introductory information	
✔ The main menu choices	
✔ The site's graphics and overall "look"	
✔ the source, or who created and pays for the site	
✔ links to other sites	

© GREAT SOURCE. ALL RIGHTS RESERVED.

NAME .... FOR USE WITH PAGES 390–403

http://www.worldseriesforkids.com/home.asp*

The World Baseball Museum presents:

World Series for Kids

An Internet Website Just for Kids!

Parents sign in here   **Kids sign in here**

World Series for Kids is a website designed with kids in mind. Here you'll find the major league stats you crave, the video clips you've been longing to see, and the best MLB Pro Shop on the World Wide Web!

Select below to browse by feature:

This Year's Series
Get ready for the game of a lifetime!

Video clips
See replays and hear analysis by the pros.

MVP facts and stats
Search our archives for fascinating facts.

Baseball bloopers
Some pictures are worth 1,000 words!

Scoreboard
Find division stats for this year and past years.

Greatest moments
Pro baseball at its finest!

Find a player
Click here to find a favorite player's website.

Link to the MLB
Find out more about Major League Baseball.

Click here to visit
BaseballforKids Pro Shop
featuring
Official World Series Merchandise

BaseballforKids is sponsored by the World Baseball Museum, a not-for-profit corporation located in Cooperstown, New York. Verne Jackson, former president of the Baseball League of America, is director of the site. Direct your comments and questions for Mr. Jackson to:
vernejackson@worldbaseballmuseum.com/

Last updated: September 2002

*URL is not real

© GREAT SOURCE. ALL RIGHTS RESERVED.

Internet

C Plan

Here are two important questions to ask yourself when reading a website:

- Does the site have the information I need? (If it doesn't, choose another.)

- Can I trust the information I find? (Some sites give opinions, not facts.)

- **Use the strategy of reading critically to examine the information posted at the site. Then decide whether the information is reliable.**

During Reading

Write your purpose questions on a 3 x 5 card. Keep the card in front of you as you explore the website.

D Read with a Purpose

A Website Profiler gives basic information about a website. It can help you understand and evaluate the most important elements of the website. Understanding and evaluating are an important part of reading critically.

© GREAT SOURCE. ALL RIGHTS RESERVED.

Directions: Carefully read the World Series for Kids website on page 167. Record your notes on the Website Profiler that follows.

Website Profiler

Name

Address (URL)

Purpose	Content Tell what the site is about here.
Graphics	Expertise Write the names of important people who work on the site here.
Sponsor Write who sponsors the site here.	Site Last Updated

Special Features

Write what you want to remember about the site here.

Internet

© GREAT SOURCE. ALL RIGHTS RESERVED.

Using the Strategy

When you read critically, you examine key information that can help you decide whether a site is reliable.

• **Use a 5 W's and H Organizer to keep track of key facts on the website.**

Directions: Write notes about the World Series website on this organizer.

5 W's and H Organizer

Subject:

Who?

Where?

Why?

What?

How?

When?

Understanding How Websites Are Organized

If you were to draw a picture of a website, you'd find that it really does look like a web. The "spokes" that reach out from the center of the web are paths or "links" that you can follow to other places on the site or on the Internet.

© GREAT SOURCE. ALL RIGHTS RESERVED.

Directions: Complete this Web. List three important links on the
World Series website. Then predict what you think you'll find there.

◆ **Web**

What I might find:
....
....
....
....
....

What I might find:
....
....
....
....
....

Link to this year's Series

Link to

World Series for kids website

Link to

Link to

What I might find:
....
....
....
....
....

What I might find:
....
....
....
....
....

© GREAT SOURCE. ALL RIGHTS RESERVED.

E Connect

Your personal opinion about a website is important. Ask yourself, "How can I use what I've learned? Should I check other sites on the Internet, or is there enough information at this site?"

- **Be sure to think about whether the website was of use to you.**

Directions: Write your reactions to the World Series for Kids website in your journal.

◄ **Journal Entry**

....
....
....

After Reading

Take your time when doing research on the Internet. First, understand what is offered on a site's home page. Then link from the home page to other sites.

F Pause and Reflect

Spend a moment reflecting on your original reading purpose.

- **After you visit a website, ask yourself, "How well did I meet my purpose? What else do I need to find out?"**

Directions: Write four facts about the World Series for Kids website on the lines below. If you can't think of four, you may need to do some rereading.

Fact #1 ....

Fact #2 ....

Fact #3 ....

Fact #4 ....

© GREAT SOURCE. ALL RIGHTS RESERVED.

G Reread

Very often you'll need to return to a site to double-check a fact or explore a link. You may also want to take a second look if you're not sure that the site is completely reliable.

• **A powerful rereading strategy to use with websites is skimming.**

Directions: Use the strategy of skimming to help you answer the questions on this organizer.

◄ Website Profiler

What is the source of the site?	What credentials does the site offer?	What is the purpose of the site?

These are the questions you should ask yourself when checking to see if a website is reliable.

© GREAT SOURCE. ALL RIGHTS RESERVED.

Internet

H Remember

Good Internet researchers remember where they've been and what they've learned.

- **To remember what you've learned, write an email to a friend.**

Directions: Write an email to a friend in which you recommend the World Series website. Tell what the site has to offer and the ways in which it was helpful.

Email

© GREAT SOURCE. ALL RIGHTS RESERVED.

Reading Tables and Graphs

To read a table or graph, first look at the "picture." Next, read the text. Then, figure out what the information means. The reading process can help.

Before Reading

A table is a listing that shows information. A graph is a type of chart. It shows the relationship between numbers or amounts. It can also show changes over time.

A Set a Purpose

Set your purpose before reading. Ask yourself these two general questions: "What is the graphic about?" and "What conclusions can I draw from it?"

- **To set your purpose, ask two or more general questions about the table or graph.**

Directions: You will be reading one table and one graph. The first shows donut preferences in the general population. The second gives information about popular pets. Write two purpose questions for each graphic on the lines below.

Graph purpose question #1: ....

....

Graph purpose question #2: ....

....

Chart purpose question #1: ....

....

Chart purpose question #2: ....

....

© GREAT SOURCE. ALL RIGHTS RESERVED.

Graphics

B Preview

At the preview stage, take a careful look at the "picture" the graphic presents.

• **Previewing can give you a general sense of what the graphic is about.**

Directions: Preview the bar graph and chart that follow. Make notes on the stickies.

Bar Graph

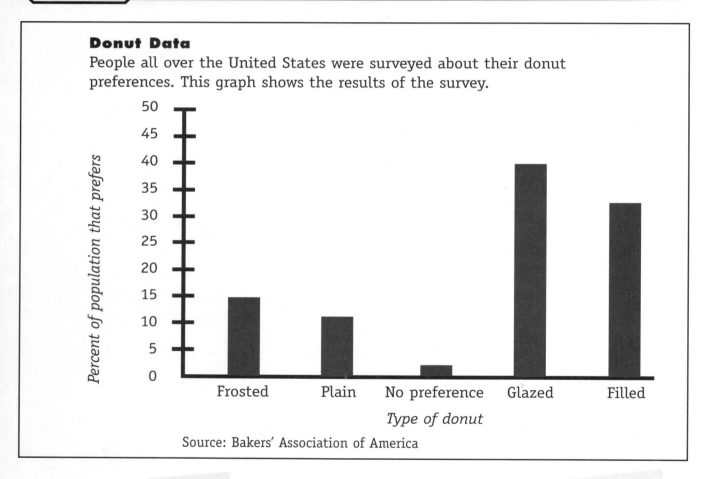

Donut Data

People all over the United States were surveyed about their donut preferences. This graph shows the results of the survey.

Percent of population that prefers

Type of donut

Source: Bakers' Association of America

The title of the bar graph is:
....
....
....

The source for the graphic is:
....
....
....

The graph shows:
....
....
....

© GREAT SOURCE. ALL RIGHTS RESERVED.

◄ Table

Parade of Pets

**Children from each grade at Tri-State Charter were asked:
"Which type or types of pets do you have?"**

Here are the results.

Grade	Dog	Cat	Fish	Bird	Snake
1	15	12	5	2	0
2	15	14	6	1	0
3	14	9	8	3	1
4	16	9	8	1	2
5	16	8	7	1	2

Source: *www.petsforkids.com*

The title of the table is:

The source for the graphic is:

The table shows:

Graphics

© GREAT SOURCE. ALL RIGHTS RESERVED.

 **Plan**

Your job when reading a graphic is to understand the information
that is presented and then figure out what it means. The strategy
of paraphrasing can make your job easier.

• **Use the strategy of paraphrasing to help you analyze the
information presented in the graphic.**

Paraphrasing means using your own words to explain the most
important details on the chart or graph.

During Reading

D Read with a Purpose

Now do a careful reading of the bar graph and chart. Remember to
take notes. The act of writing can make it easier for you to "absorb"
the most important details.

Directions: Make notes about the two graphics on these charts.

Paraphrase Chart

Notes: Donut Bar Graph	My Paraphrase
The subject is:	
Key fact:	
Key fact:	
My thoughts:	

© GREAT SOURCE. ALL RIGHTS RESERVED.

NAME

Paraphrase Chart

Notes: Pet Chart	My Paraphrase
The subject is:	
Key fact:	
Key fact:	
My thoughts:	

Using the Strategy

You can use several different tools when paraphrasing. If a Paraphrase Chart doesn't work, try creating Summary Notes.

• **Summary Notes can help you draw conclusions about the information presented in a chart or graph.**

Directions: Write Summary Notes about the two graphics you just read.

Summary Notes

Title Donut Data	Write what you think is the main point or idea here.
Main Point	
Detail 1	
Detail 2	
Detail 3	

List three smaller details that support the main idea here.

Graphics

© GREAT SOURCE. ALL RIGHTS RESERVED.

Summary Notes

Title Parade of Pets

Main Point

> Write what you think is the main point or idea here.

Detail 1

Detail 2

Detail 3

> List three smaller details that support the main idea here.

Understanding How Graphics Are Organized

Understanding the most important facts and details in a graphic is key to unlocking what it says.

Directions: Label these elements on the graphic below: *title, information, source, horizontal (x) axis,* and *vertical (y) axis.* If needed, review the definitions for these terms on pages 414–415, 419, and 426 of your handbook.

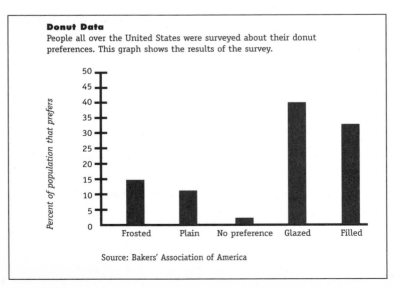

Donut Data
People all over the United States were surveyed about their donut preferences. This graph shows the results of the survey.

Percent of population that prefers

Frosted   Plain   No preference   Glazed   Filled

Source: Bakers' Association of America

© GREAT SOURCE. ALL RIGHTS RESERVED.

Connect

It's always interesting to make a personal connection to a graphic. This too can strengthen your understanding of the facts.

- **Use a Double-entry Journal to respond to information in a graphic.**

Directions: Write your thoughts and feelings about the graphics you've just read.

Double-entry Journal

Graphics	My Thoughts and Feelings
Donut Data	
Parade of Pets	

© GREAT SOURCE. ALL RIGHTS RESERVED.

Graphics

After Reading

Always return to a graphic for a second look to be sure that you've interpreted the results correctly.

F Pause and Reflect

First, think back to your reading purpose. See if you can answer both questions.

• **After you finish a selection, ask yourself, "How well did I meet my purpose?"**

Directions: Answer your reading purpose questions.

Graph purpose question #1: ....
                                    My question

....

....
                                    My answer

Graph purpose question #2: ....
                                    My question

....

....
                                    My answer

Chart purpose question #1: ....
                                    My question

....

....
                                    My answer

Chart purpose question #2: ....
                                    My question

....

....
                                    My answer

© GREAT SOURCE. ALL RIGHTS RESERVED.

Reread

Reread a graphic for facts you missed the first time around. Do these facts change the conclusions you've drawn?

• **The rereading strategy of close reading can help you draw some additional conclusions about a graphic.**

Directions: Draw some additional conclusions about the donut graph. Do the same for the pet chart. Refer to page 522 in your handbook if you get stuck.

Summary Notes

Steps for Drawing Conclusions	Donut Data Graph
What is being compared or classified in the graphic?	
Compare the data. What similarities and differences do you see?	
Think about what's shown. Is there anything unusual about the way the data are presented? Is anything left out?	
What trends or other relationships do you see?	

© GREAT SOURCE. ALL RIGHTS RESERVED.

Graphics

Summary Notes

Steps for Drawing Conclusions	Parade of Pets Chart
What is being compared or classified in the graphic?	
Compare the data. What similarities and differences do you see?	
Think about what's shown. Is there anything unusual about the way the data is presented? Is anything left out?	
What trends or other relationships do you see?	

 Remember

It's easy to remember a graphic if you actually *do* something with the information.

• To remember a graphic, make a list.

Directions: Make a list of facts and details you learned from reading the donut bar graph. Do the same for the pets chart.

Journal Entry

What I learned from the donut bar graph	What I learned from the pets chart

© GREAT SOURCE. ALL RIGHTS RESERVED.

Reading a Test and Test Questions

Some of the tests you take in school will be pretty challenging. You'll have to prepare well and stay focused. On the day of the test, you'll need to read carefully and use the strategies you learned in the handbook.

Before Reading

Your goal for any test is to get the answers right. Setting a purpose before you begin can help you meet this goal.

A Set a Purpose

Your purpose is to understand what the test questions are asking and figure out what information is needed for the answers.

• **To set your purpose, ask a question about the test.**

<u>Directions:</u> On the pages that follow, you'll read an excerpt from a novel and then answer some questions about the reading. Write your purpose on the lines below.

My purpose:

....

....

....

....

© GREAT SOURCE. ALL RIGHTS RESERVED.

Tests

B Preview

Always spend a moment or two previewing the test before you begin. Try to get a sense of what the reading is about and what the test questions are like.

Directions: Preview the test that follows. Make some notes on the preview stickies.

Mid-year Reading Test

Mid-year Reading Test
60 Minutes—4 questions, 1 Essay
DIRECTIONS: Read this excerpt from the novel *Hope Was Here*. Then answer the questions that follow.
Mid-Year Review, Passage

"Job Change" from *Hope Was Here* by Joan Bauer

Somehow I knew my time had come when Bambi Barnes tore her order book into little pieces, hurled it in the air like confetti, and got fired from the Rainbow Diner in Pensacola right in the middle of the lunchtime rush. She'd been sobbing by the decaf urn, having accidentally spilled a bowl of navy bean soup in the lap of a man who was, as we say in the restaurant game, one taco short of a combo platter. Gib, the day manager, was screaming at her to stop crying, which made her cry all the more, which led to the firing and her stomping out the door wailing how life wasn't fair, right in front of the hungry customers. That's when Gib turned to me.

"You want her job?"

I was a bus girl at the time, which meant I cleaned off dirty tables and brought people water and silverware. I'd been salivating for years to be a waitress.

I stood up tall, "Yes, I sure do."

"You going to cry on me, fall apart if something goes wrong?"

And I saw right then if you're going to cut the mustard in food service, you'd better know how to

Preview
How much time do you have to complete the test?

Preview
What do you learn about the questions?

Preview
What is the reading passage about?

© GREAT SOURCE. ALL RIGHTS RESERVED.

Mid-year Reading Test, continued

handle turmoil. I straightened my shoulders, did my best to look like flint.

"I'm the toughest female you've ever seen," I assured him.

"You're hired then. Take the counter."

Multiple-choice Questions

DIRECTIONS: Read each question and decide which choice is the correct answer. There is no penalty for incorrect answers. This means that it is better to make a guess than leave the question blank.

1. "Job Change" is told from the point of view of:
   A. a diner chef.
   B. a diner bus girl.
   C. a diner bus boy.
   D. a diner customer.

2. Based on the reading, which of these statements is not true?
   A. The narrator longs to be more than just a waitress.
   B. The narrator is eager to take Bambi's job.
   C. The narrator is strong-willed.
   D. The narrator considers herself to be "tough."

During Reading

What are the key words or phrases in this question?

_____

During Reading

What is this question asking me for?

_____

_____

_____

Tests

© GREAT SOURCE. ALL RIGHTS RESERVED.

Mid-year Reading Test, continued

3. The phrase "one taco short of a combo platter" is an example of:
   A. a main idea.
   B. a simile.
   C. a metaphor.
   D. an idiom.

During Reading

What strategy will I use to answer this question?

....

....

....

4. What is the mood of the excerpt?
   A. sad
   B. thoughtful
   C. humorous
   D. angry

During Reading

How I figured out the answer:

....

....

....

Essay Question

5. Tell about a job you've had. It can be a job that you were hired for or one that you volunteered to do. Describe what the job was like and how you felt about it. Be sure to tell what you learned from the experience.

During Reading

What will be the topic of the essay?

....

....

....

© GREAT SOURCE. ALL RIGHTS RESERVED.

NAME ....

Plan

After your preview, make a plan. First, decide how much time to spend on each section of the test.

Directions: How much time will you need to complete each part of the sample test? Make notes on the chart.

▶ Planning Chart

What to Do	Time I'll Spend

> Keep these time limits in mind as you take the test.

During Reading

D Read with a Purpose

Always allow enough time for two careful readings of the test passage and questions. Take notes as you go.

Directions: Read "Job Change." Underline one or two important sentences in each paragraph.

Using the Strategy

Next, choose a strategy that can help you find answers to the test questions.

- **Use the strategy of skimming to help you read and respond to items on a test.**

When you skim, you let your eyes travel down a page. You pause when your eyes "catch" an important word or phrase.

Directions: Read the four multiple-choice test questions on pages 187 and 188. Circle the correct answers. Make notes on the stickies.

© GREAT SOURCE. ALL RIGHTS RESERVED.

Tests

Understanding How Tests Are Organized

On most tests, the easy questions come first, and the more challenging questions come later. These challenging questions are often "open response" or essay-type questions.

Directions: Reread the essay question that follows "Job Change." Make notes on the sticky. On the lines below, explain what the essay question is asking you to do.

The essay question is asking me to

....

....

 **Connect**

As often as possible, try to make a personal connection to a test passage. Connecting can make the passage easier to understand.

• **You can use your own thoughts and feelings to help you answer the questions on a test.**

Directions: Plan your essay on the organizer below. First, write a sentence that tells your main idea. Then write three details that support the main idea.

Main Idea Organizer

Main Idea		
Detail 1	**Detail 2**	**Detail 3**

© GREAT SOURCE. ALL RIGHTS RESERVED.

After Reading

Save a couple of minutes at the end of the test to check your work.

F Pause and Reflect

As a first step, run your eyes down the answer sheet. Be sure you've answered every question.

- **Ask yourself, "Have I answered each question to the best of my ability?"**

This is the multiple-choice question that I found most difficult: ....

Here's why: ....

....

G Reread

Checking your answers means rereading specific parts of the passage.

- **A powerful rereading strategy to use is visualizing and thinking aloud.**

Directions: Reread and check your multiple-choice answers. Then exchange books with a friend and "grade" each other's work.

H Remember

When your teacher returns your graded test, examine it carefully. Figure out what you did wrong so that you can avoid making the same mistakes on future exams.

- **Remember the test questions that gave you trouble.**

Directions: Write three things *you* can do to improve your test-taking abilities.

I can improve my test-taking abilities by ....

....

....

© GREAT SOURCE. ALL RIGHTS RESERVED.

Tests

Focus on Writing for Tests

Writing tests measure how well you can organize your ideas and how well you can use the rules of proper English. It pays to have a plan in mind.

Step 1: Read the directions.

First, read the directions at least twice.

Directions: Read these writing test directions. Highlight key words. Then make notes on the stickies.

Sample Writing Test
DIRECTIONS: Write a description of a favorite person, place, or thing. Write at least three details that support your description. Remember to proofread your writing.

What type of essay will you write?

What is the topic of the writing?

Step 2: Plan your writing.

Next, choose a topic. Then plan the essay on an organizer.

Directions: Make notes about your essay on the following organizer.

Main Idea Organizer

Topic		
Topic Sentence		
Detail 1	**Detail 2**	**Detail 3**

© GREAT SOURCE. ALL RIGHTS RESERVED.

Step 3: Write your essay.

Your next step is to write your essay. Refer to your organizer as you write.

Directions: Write the first paragraph of your favorite person, place, or thing description here.

....

....

....

....

....

....

....

Step 4: Check your writing.

As a final step, proofread your writing. First, reread the essay. Make sure it has plenty of details. Then correct any spelling mistakes and problems with punctuation and capitalization.

Directions: Proofread the paragraph you just wrote. Make your corrections neatly. Then make some notes about your writing on the lines below.

Here's how I can improve my writing: ....

....

....

....

....

....

© GREAT SOURCE. ALL RIGHTS RESERVED.

Focus on Math Tests

You can use the tools and strategies in the Reader's Handbook *to help you with a math test. Here's how.*

Step 1: Read the directions and the questions.

First read the test directions. Then read the questions one at a time. Underline key words and make notes in the margin.

Directions: Read the directions and the sample problem. Highlight key words.

> **Sample Math Test Question**
>
> **DIRECTIONS:** Read each problem. Circle the letter of the correct answer. You may make notes in the margin of the test booklet.
> 1. Tino bought a new game system for $199.00 and 3 new games at $49.99 each. He paid 6% tax on his purchases. How much did Tino spend altogether?
> A. $438.77   C. $348.97
> B. $398.61   D. $369.91
>
> **Highlight key words in the directions and problem.**

Step 2: Decide how to solve the problem.

Use the strategy of thinking aloud to figure out how to solve the problem.

Directions: Write a Think Aloud that tells how you would solve the sample test question.

Think Aloud

....

....

....

....

© GREAT SOURCE. ALL RIGHTS RESERVED.

NAME ....

Step 3: Solve and check.

Finish by solving the problem and checking your work. If you get stuck, try visualizing and solving the problem with easier numbers.

Directions: Make a sketch that shows what the sample problem is asking for. Write your answer at the bottom of the sketch.

© GREAT SOURCE. ALL RIGHTS RESERVED.

Focus on Science Tests

Use your critical reading skills to improve your performance on a science test.

Step 1: Read the question.

Always do at least two careful readings of each question. Mark key words and phrases.

Directions: Read this sample question. Highlight the key words. Then make notes on the sticky.

Sample Science Test Question

1. Which of these does not occur during hibernation?
    A. the heartbeat slows
    B. the body hardly moves
    C. the body burns stored fat
    D. the appetite increases

For question #1, I need

to figure out

Step 2: Find the answer.

Next, use the strategy of thinking aloud to talk your way through to the answer.

Directions: Read the answer choices for the hibernation question. Write a Think Aloud that tells how to figure out the answer.

Think Aloud

To find the answer,

_____

_____

The correct answer is

© GREAT SOURCE. ALL RIGHTS RESERVED.

Step 3: Draw conclusions from the graphics.

When you come to a graphics question, first take a look at the "big picture." Then read the graphic's text. Finish by answering the question or questions.

Directions: Read the graphic. Make notes on the stickies. Then answer the question and explain your choice.

Sample Science Test Question

Size of the Six Continents

Continent	Area (million square miles)
North America	9.4
South America	6.9
Eurasia	21.2
Africa	11.7
Australia	3.3
Antarctica	5.4

2. What is the correct conclusion to draw from the data on the chart?
    A. Three of the continents are approximately the same size.
    B. Eurasia is the largest continent.
    C. Africa is twice as large as Eurasia.
    D. North America is 9.4 billion square miles.

The test question asks me to

figure

To answer the question, I will

The title of the

graphic is

It shows

The answer is

because

Tests

© GREAT SOURCE. ALL RIGHTS RESERVED.

Focus on Social Studies Tests

Social studies tests examine your knowledge of names, dates, and events in history. Reading critically is key to performing well. Here is a plan that can help.

Step 1: Read the question.

Always answer the easier questions first. But no matter how easy the question seems, read it carefully.

Directions: Read this sample test question. Highlight the key words.

> **Sample Social Studies Test Question**
>
> 1. Who was John Brown?
>   A. a founder of the Antislavery Society
>   B. a wealthy plantation owner who opposed slavery
>   C. a Philadelphia Quaker minister
>   D. a white abolitionist who organized an attack on Harpers Ferry

Step 2: Talk your way through the answers.

Eliminate answers that you know are wrong. Then use the strategy of thinking aloud to talk your way through to an answer.

Directions: Read the answer choices for the John Brown question. Then write a Think Aloud that tells how you will figure out the answer.

> **Think Aloud**

I know _____ and _____ are wrong because _____

....

....

....

....

© GREAT SOURCE. ALL RIGHTS RESERVED.

NAME ....

Step 3: Draw conclusions from the graphics.

When you come to a graphics question, begin by looking at the "big picture." Then read the graphic's text and use what you've learned to answer the question.

Directions: Read the bar graph and the question. Make notes on the stickies.

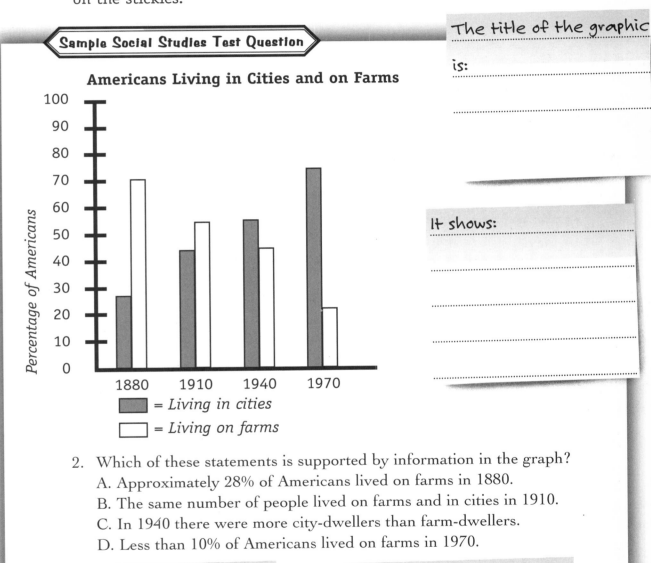

Sample Social Studies Test Question

Americans Living in Cities and on Farms

Percentage of Americans

1880 1910 1940 1970

▨ = *Living in cities*
▢ = *Living on farms*

The title of the graphic is:
....
....

It shows:
....
....
....
....

2. Which of these statements is supported by information in the graph?
   A. Approximately 28% of Americans lived on farms in 1880.
   B. The same number of people lived on farms and in cities in 1910.
   C. In 1940 there were more city-dwellers than farm-dwellers.
   D. Less than 10% of Americans lived on farms in 1970.

To answer question # 2, I need to:
....
....
....

The correct answer is:
....
....
....

© GREAT SOURCE. ALL RIGHTS RESERVED.

Tests

Learning New Words

Learning new words can help you be a better reader, a better speaker, and even a better thinker. Here is a plan that you can use to improve your vocabulary.

Step 1: Read.

When you come to an unfamiliar word in your reading, take the time to "collect" it.

Directions: Read this passage from a famous novel. Circle words that are unfamiliar to you.

> **from *The Slave Dancer* by Paula Fox**
>
> Except for the wooden sewing box, a sea chest which had belonged to my mother's father, and her work table, we owned scarcely anything. One cupboard held the few scraps of our linen, the cooking pots and implements, candle ends and a bottle of burning liquid which my mother rubbed on Betty's chest when she was feverish. There were two chamber pots on the floor, hidden by day in the shadow of the cupboard but clearly visible by candlelight, the white porcelain one chipped and discolored, the other decorated with a painting of an ugly orange flower which my mother said was a lily.

Step 2: Record.

Keep a running list of words you don't know. Add to the list over the course of the school year. Remember to record where you first noticed the unfamiliar words.

© GREAT SOURCE. ALL RIGHTS RESERVED.

Directions: In the left column of the chart, write the words you circled.

Reading Journal

	Unfamiliar Words	Definitions
●	1. scarcely	

Step 3: Define.

Try defining the unfamiliar words using context clues. If that doesn't work, use a dictionary.

Directions: Get together with a partner. Working together, define the words on your list. Then define the words on your partner's list.

Step 4: Use the words.

The best way to remember a new word is to use it in conversation or in writing.

Directions: Working with your partner, write one sentence for each of the words you defined. Your sentences should make it clear that you understand the definitions of the words.

Practice Sentences

....

....

....

....

....

....

© GREAT SOURCE. ALL RIGHTS RESERVED.

Vocabulary

Building Vocabulary

There are two strategies you can use to define an unknown word. The first is context clues. The second involves using word parts.

Step 1: Use context clues.

Using context clues means searching surrounding sentences for hints about the unknown word.

Directions: Review pages 500–503 in your handbook for information about using context clues. Then read the short passage below. Use context clues to figure out the meaning of the underlined words.

from *Pocho* by José Antonio Villarreal

It was spring in Santa Clara. The empty lots were green with new grass, and at the edge of town, where the orchards began their <u>indiscernible</u> rise to the end of the valley floor and halfway up the foothills of the Diablo Range, the ground was blanketed with cherry blossoms, which, <u>nudged</u> from their perch by a clean, soft breeze, floated down like gentle snow. A child walked through an empty lot, not looking back, for the <u>wake</u> of trampled grass he created made him sad.

Underlined Words	My Definition	Context Clues
indiscernible		
nudged		
wake		

© GREAT SOURCE. ALL RIGHTS RESERVED.

Step 2: Use word parts.

If context clues don't work, try using word parts. These are roots, prefixes, and suffixes.

Directions: Complete this word tree. Add words with the root *duc*.

Root Words

duc = lead

conduct

Directions: Add a prefix from the box to each of the words on the list. Then tell what the word means.

Prefixes

dis- = the reverse of	*fore-* = previously, in front of, away from	*mid-* = middle

Prefix + Word	New Word	Meaning of New Word
+ agree		
+ fathers		
+ term		

Directions: Add suffixes to these words. Then use each word in a sentence.

Suffixes

-ness = a state of	*-ward* = in the direction of

restless + -ness =   Sentence:

east + -ward =   Sentence:

© GREAT SOURCE. ALL RIGHTS RESERVED.

Vocabulary

203

Dictionary Dipping

Learning the parts of a dictionary can make finding a word easier and faster.

Step 1: Read.

Review "Use a Dictionary" on pages 508–509 in your handbook.

Directions: Read this sample dictionary entry. Then answer the questions that follow.

> ### Dictionary Entry
>
> indices • Indochina
>
> **indifferent** (in-di´-fərnt) *adj.* 1. Not partial; unbiased. 2. Not mattering one way or the other. 3. Having no marked feeling for or against. 4. Having no particular concern for; apathetic. 5. Neither good nor bad; mediocre. — indifference *n.* —indifferently *adv.*

How many definitions does *indifferent* have?

What part of speech is *indifferent?*

What is the noun form of the word *indifferent?*

What are some synonyms for *indifferent?*

Step 2: Remember.

The easiest way to remember a word is to use it often.

Directions: Write two sentences for the word *indifferent.*

Sentence #1:

Sentence #2:

© GREAT SOURCE. ALL RIGHTS RESERVED.

Understanding New Terms

It will be helpful for you to keep a running list of new terms over the course of a school year. Use the list to help you study for midterm or final exams.

Step 1: Record.

Use a graphic organizer such as a Concept Map to keep track of new terms and their definitions.

Directions: Take a second look at the terms listed in the Key Terms box for "Reconstruction: The First Year" (page 23). Write three of the terms on this Concept Map.

> Concept Map

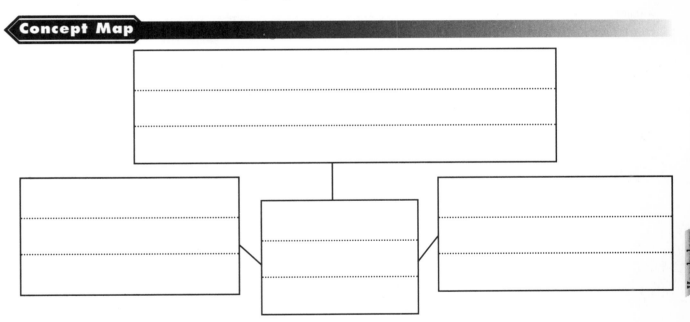

Step 2: Define.

Use context clues, word parts, and the dictionary to define each new term listed.

Directions: Define the three new terms you've recorded on your Concept Map. If you have time, add terms from "The Five Kingdoms," pages 35–37.

© GREAT SOURCE. ALL RIGHTS RESERVED.

Vocabulary

Mastering Vocabulary Tests

You'll probably take lots of vocabulary tests as a student. It's a good idea to master these tests now, before they get any harder. Here are tips that you can use with various types of vocabulary questions.

1. Definition Questions

First look for familiar roots, prefixes, and suffixes. These can give you clues about the meaning of the word in question.

Directions: Circle the correct definition for *import*. Then explain.

Sample Question

1. *Import* is
   A. carry in   C. reject
   B. put under   D. invite

This is how I figured out the answer:

2. Synonym Questions

With these types of questions, begin by looking for the base word. It may point you in the direction of the correct synonym.

Directions: Circle the correct answer. Then explain.

Sample Question

2. Which is a synonym for *summit*?
   A. the lowest point   C. the highest point
   B. the roughest point   D. the smoothest point

This is how I figured out the answer:

© GREAT SOURCE. ALL RIGHTS RESERVED.

3. Antonym Questions

You'll also look for a root or base word to help you answer antonym questions.

Directions: Circle the correct answer. Then explain.

Sample Question

3. Which is an antonym for *devoid*?
   A. disturbed   C. incompetent
   B. empty   D. filled

This is how I figured out the answer:

4. Analogy Questions

To solve an analogy question, figure out the relationship between the given words.

Directions: Read questions 4 and 5. Make notes on the stickies.

Sample Question

4. February : March :: spring :
   A. Easter
   B. fall
   C. winter
   D. summer

5. vegetable : broccoli :: animal :
   A. life
   B. feed
   C. cow
   D. barn

What is the relationship between March and February?

My answer and why:

What is the relationship between broccoli and vegetable?

My answer and why:

© GREAT SOURCE. ALL RIGHTS RESERVED.

Vocabulary

Author and Title Index

Photo Credits

24 ©Corbis

25 ©Corbis

37 *top* ©Photodisc
bottom ©Corbis/Stock Market

57 ©Photodisc

58 ©Photodisc

68 ©Corbis

100 ©Photodisc

167 ©Photodisc

© GREAT SOURCE. ALL RIGHTS RESERVED.